CHALONER OF THE BENGAL CAVALRY

CHALONER OF THE BENGAL CAVALRY

A TALE OF THE INDIAN MUTINY

PERCIVAL LANCASTER

GYAN

Published by

Gyan Publishing House
5, Ansari Road
Daryaganj, New Delhi-110002
Phone: 011-47034999, 9811692060
E-mail: books@gyanbooks.com

Distribution Network
gyanbooks.com
India, USA, Canada, UK, Australia

ISBN: 978-93-7447-034-3 (PB)

First Published, 1889

2nd Impression 2025

Printed at: Gyan Press, Delhi.

CHALONER OF THE BENGAL CAVALRY
Author: PERCIVAL LANCASTER

Chaloner of the Bengal Cavalry

C 745

CHALONER SAHIB IS SAVED BY THE ARRIVAL OF THE
BRITISH TROOPS

Chaloner of the Bengal Cavalry

A Tale of the Indian Mutiny

BY

Lieut. PERCIVAL LANCASTER, R.E.

ILLUSTRATED BY CHARLES M. SHELDON

BLACKIE AND SON LIMITED

LONDON GLASGOW AND BOMBAY

Contents

Illustrations

CHALONER OF THE BENGAL CAVALRY

CHAPTER I

The Signal

"*Khidmutgar! hi, khidmutgar!* Where has that lazy Yusufzai hidden himself now? Ho! Urghab Ali! *hitherao!* (Come here!) I require thee." Thus Lieutenant Peter Chaloner, of the Honourable East India Company's regiment of Fifth Bengal Cavalry, stationed, this ninth day of May, eighteen hundred and fifty-seven, at the military cantonment of Mirapur, some forty miles distant from Delhi, the capital city of the old King of Oudh.

Chaloner, now about nineteen years of age, had come out to India some twelve months previously, having obtained a commission in the Company's service, and, on arrival at Calcutta, had been posted to the Fifth Bengal Native Cavalry, quartered at Mirapur, where it formed the only cavalry regiment, native or otherwise, in the district. There were, however, two native infantry regiments stationed at the same place, together with a strong British force of artillery and infantry; so that the young man had not found his short term of military experience hang heavily on his hands by any means.

Unlike some others of the young officers stationed at Mirapur, Chaloner had taken great interest in his professional duties, and found plenty of occupation in the task of converting himself into a thoroughly efficient officer; with the result that he had earned the hearty praise of his colonel, and had already been brought under the notice of General Hewlitt, the District Commander. This was perhaps one of the reasons why the young lieutenant had been invited to the grand ball which was to take place that evening at General Hewlitt's house, and for which he was now dressing in the seclusion of his own little four-roomed bungalow on the Delhi road. He had mislaid his mess-dress waistcoat, and had been so long hunting for it that he was already a little behind the time set for the commencement of the dancing; and as there were several reasons—not altogether unconnected with the general's own household—why he desired to be early, he was considerably annoyed, and finally shouted angrily for his man, Urghab Ali, to come and assist in the search for the missing garment. Perhaps the fellow had taken it away to brush it, and had forgotten to bring it back, thought Chaloner; at any rate it must be found, so "Urghab Ali! Urghab Ali!" he shouted again, going out to the back veranda, and whistling in the direction of the servants' quarters.

And then a soft voice just behind him enquired: "Does the sahib require his servant? His servant is here."

"Great Scot, man, how you startled me!" exclaimed Chaloner, wheeling round as if shot. "Of course I want you. I've been shouting for you these ten minutes past. Where have you been, you—you Pathan?"

Urghab Ali grinned. He knew that his master was

merely pretending to be angry, and that Chaloner's bark was, to him, always much worse than his bite.

"To the bazar, heaven-born," he replied, saluting. "Does not the sahib remember that he gave me leave so to do, provided I returned by sunset?"

"So I did," answered the lieutenant, smiling. "And as the sun has only been below the horizon for about an hour, I suppose I must excuse you. But look here, Urghab, where's my mess waistcoat? I've hunted everywhere for it, and can't find it. Have you taken it away to clean it, or anything? I want the thing at once, for I'm already overdue at General Hewlitt's place."

The Pathan scratched his black mane and looked slowly round the room.

"No, sahib," he replied, "I have not seen it. Has the sahib looked in the tin uniform-case?"

"Confound it all, no," admitted Chaloner, striding over to the corner where the case stood. "What a fool I am, to be sure! That's the only place I didn't search, and—yes, of course, here it is. Now, Urghab, give it a brush, and the jacket as well; and put a little extra polish on those spurs while I wash.

"So you've been to the bazar again, eh?" he continued, soaping himself vigorously. "Any more rumours like the last flying about, or are things simmering down?"

Urghab Ali's smiling face assumed a serious and rather stern expression as he replied: "No, heaven-born, things are not quieting down; quite the contrary. And there are many rumours in the bazar; one of which is, that the *Râj* of the sahibs is fast drawing to its close, and that it will come to an end amid whirlwinds of fire and rivers of blood! I tell thee, sahib, I like it not at all. Those *soors* of bazar-born *badmâshes* speak with too much confidence for my liking; they speak as if they *knew*, as if they were sure; and—hast not thyself noticed how the behaviour of the *sowârs* and sepoys has altered for the worse during the last few months? Once they obeyed all orders unquestioningly; now they sometimes hesitate—even do they sometimes give the sahibs back look for look, word for word; and it is in my mind that ere long they will refuse to obey altogether, and then, sahib—then——"

"Cease thy prattle, thou old croaker," laughed Chaloner, towelling his dripping body. "To hear thee talk, one would indeed believe that the end of the British rule in India was at hand. Why, man, there are always rumours in the bazars, some favourable to us, some unfavourable. I myself know that 'tis said we have been thrashed by the Russians in the Crimea, and by the Persians at Herât, yet did any lift a hand to rescue them when we marched those eighty-five men to the jail to-day, after stripping their uniforms and arms from them? On the twenty-fourth of last month they refused, like the ignorant fools they are, to bite their cartridges, for fear of being defiled; and what has been the result? Degradation, and a sentence of ten years' imprisonment! No, no, Urghab; our rule is not at an end, or anything like it, when we can have our commands carried out as they were to-day. Think ye that, if disaffection were as rampant as ye seem to suppose, my *sowârs* of the Fifth would have stood by and seen their comrades shamed, and afterwards acted as their guard to the jail? They would not, and well thou knowest it. Thou art an old woman, Urghab."

The Pathan shrugged his shoulders, and helped his master to finish dressing.

"Time will show, sahib," he said. "But remember that men who seek a great revenge may put up with slight and insult for a time, in order to further their own plans and make their revenge more complete. And when the time comes for the flame to break forth, it may prove all the fiercer for being pent up so long; so heed thy servant's words and—beware! The time may be nearer than any of us think. Goes the other young sahib, thy friend, also to the house of the general to-night?"

"Neville Fairbanks Sahib? Yes, he goes," answered Chaloner. "Why enquirest thou?"

"He belongeth to the Telegraph, is it not so?"

"Yes; but why these questions, Urghab?"

"Tell him," replied the Pathan, "that, if trouble should come, he had better not try to send the news by the wires that speak, for if he does he will be killed. The *dâk* (post office) is the first place they will make for."

"'They?' Whom dost thou mean by 'they', Urghab?" asked the lieutenant. "Thou art speaking in riddles."

"The riddle is easily read, heaven-born," retorted Urghab; "I mean the mutineers, the rebel sepoys, the revolted Company's army—yes, the whole native army."

Chaloner wheeled round, facing the Pathan, his eyes gleaming with anger. "Thou windbag," he exclaimed, "thou retailer of bazar gossip, thou art crazy! Dream not for a moment that the native army is disloyal. Some dissatisfaction there may be about the matter of the greased cartridge, but the proclamation of the *sirkar* (Government), that neither the fat of cows nor that of pigs goes to the making of the tallow smeared on the cartridges, will soon put an end to that storm in a tea-cup. There certainly does seem some possibility of a rising, or rather disturbance, among a few of the more ignorant of the population, the *badmâshes*, but the army will put an end to anything of that kind before it gets a chance even to raise its head. No, no, Urghab, get that idea out of your mind; heed not the example of those men we took to jail to-day. There are black sheep in every army—they are the few exceptions to the rule that the native army is loyal to us and will stand by us in every emergency."

The Pathan sighed. "Well, sahib," he said, "I have spoken my warning, and if thou wilt not believe, I can do no more. But time will show who is right, thou or I; and believe this, sahib, whatever else thou dost disbelieve when the storm breaks, thou wilt find one faithful sword at thy call—ay, two. The *subâhdar* of thy regiment, Shere Singh, he will stand by thee too, for he loves thee even as do I; and we three together may save our own lives and those of others, where one alone would fail. Do not forget, sahib; when the need arises, Shere Singh and I will hasten to thy side."

"I will not forget, old war-dog," said Chaloner, laying his hand affectionately on the man's shoulder. "I verily believe that thou wouldst welcome war, if only to feel thy fingers round the hilt of a *tulwâr* once again. This life must seem tame to thee, after thy fights up in the Yusufzai hills in thy young days."

"I care not, heaven-born," returned the old man, fixing his hawk-like eyes on his master, "so long as I may be with thee. I served thy father—on whose head be peace!—before thee, and thee too will I serve until I die."

At this moment the sound of a horse's hoofs and the rattle of wheels was heard coming along the road, to stop a few seconds later opposite the door of the bungalow, while a clear young voice rang out: "I say, Peter, are you still there; and do you know what time it is?"

"There is Fairbanks Sahib now," smiled the Pathan.

"Shall I go out and hold the horse, heaven-born, or art thou ready?"

"I'm ready, I think, Urghab," replied Chaloner, looking hurriedly round the room. "Go thou and tell the sahib I shall be with him in a minute."

The old fellow saluted and went to the garden gate, where Chaloner presently heard the two men talking together.

Finding that he had at last got himself garbed to his liking, the young man flung his military cloak round his shoulders, ran out of the house, and clambered into the dog-cart which his friend had brought to fetch him.

"All right, Urghab!" he cried, as he tucked the driving robe round his knees. "You need not wait up for me, as I shall probably be late; but put out a snack to eat and some beer or something, for two, as Fairbanks Sahib will perhaps stay the night with me. Let go the horse's head."

"It shall be done, heaven-born," answered Urghab, and stood aside as the carriage containing the two chums wheeled round and sped away in the beautiful tropic moonlight. As long as it remained in view he stood at the gate watching, and when it disappeared round a bend in the road he shook his head slowly and sadly, as though oppressed by a sense of foreboding, and strode gloomily back to the house.

Neville Fairbanks, a youth in the Telegraph Department, who had been born in India and had lived there the whole of his short life of seventeen years, was Chaloner's greatest chum at Mirapur. He had taken to the young officer immediately upon his arrival at the station, and had cultivated his acquaintance until the two had become fast friends; Chaloner deriving a great deal of benefit from his chum's Indian experience, while Fairbanks was never tired of hearing about that Mother-country over the seas, whose white and green beauty it had never been his privilege to gaze upon.

Personally the two youngsters were somewhat similar in appearance, except that the officer looked a good deal older than his years, and consequently than Fairbanks, who did not seem more than about sixteen. Both were dark, Fairbanks almost to swarthiness through long exposure to the Indian sun; both were of about the same height, namely five feet nine or ten inches; both had very dark, curly hair; and both were singularly handsome lads. Chaloner took great pride in a short, crisp beard and moustache, which added to his appearance of maturity, and which was the cause of unending envy to his chum, who was doing his utmost to induce a moustache of his own by carefully shaving the down on his upper lip with scrupulous regularity every day. Their temperaments also were very similar, both having an extremely strong sense of justice and an instinctive repugnance to anything not quite "straight"; and both were hot-headed, eager, and impulsive to a degree, generous to a fault, and great favourites among all with whom they came into contact.

Such were the lads who, had they but known it, were within a few hours of entering upon a period of blood, fire, and cruelty such as even India itself had never yet known. But for the present they were mercifully oblivious to the scenes and experiences awaiting them, and drove happily along the road toward General Hewlitt's house, where they anticipated a thoroughly enjoyable evening, laughing and talking merrily as they went.

"Bit late, aren't you?" Fairbanks enquired as soon as he had managed to convince his horse that he was not competing in a race round the *Maidan* (park).

"Yes," returned Chaloner, glancing at his watch, "I am afraid I am. I couldn't find some of my things until old Urghab came back from the bazar, and then the silly beggar kept me there chatting until I forgot all about the time. And I say, old man," he went on, as the dog-cart whirled round a corner, "that Yusufzai of mine certainly has a queer bee in his bonnet this time. He's always full of weird ideas, as you know, but what do you think is the latest? He's got it into his head, somehow, that the little bit of trouble we've been having lately is merely the forerunner to—a revolt of the whole native army! How's that for a yarn? Idiotic, isn't it?" And he laughed light-heartedly.

But to Chaloner's great surprise his friend did not echo his merriment; instead, when Peter turned to look at him, he saw that Fairbanks's face showed a little pale in the moonlight, and that his lips were closed in a thin, scarlet line.

"I'm not so sure," asserted Fairbanks, observing his friend's questioning glance. "As a matter of fact I was only waiting until we arrived at the general's to have a chat with you on that particular subject. Personally I believe, Pete, that we *are* on the eve of some very terrible catastrophe. I am not quite so old as you, but I have lived in India all my life, and I think I know the native mind as well as it is possible for any European to know it. I tell you candidly, old man, I do not at all like the look of things. There are many, very many signs—which it would take too long to explain to a new-comer like yourself—that go to prove to me that things are not at all what they should be—no, not by a great deal. Your motto is: 'Never believe bazar rumour'; mine is: 'Always pay attention to it'; for the truth is invariably to be found there, if you only know how to seek for it. Bazar rumour says that the British *Râj* is nearly at an end, and I have a very strong suspicion that the native army is determined to make a certain old prophecy come true. Yes, you may stare. You officers all swear by your men, and say that, whoever else should fail, your sepoys will always remain loyal. But—*don't be too sure!* Over-confidence in your men may mean plunging India into such a chaos of murder, strife, and sudden death as the country has never known; so take my advice and be on your guard. I only wish that any words of mine could awaken the general officers to facts; but I know it's no use. I might as well save my breath; for nothing on this earth, save revolt itself, will ever convince a British officer that his sepoys are not everything that is best and noblest."

"Heavens, Neville, what are you saying?" exclaimed Chaloner, horrified. "Have you any proof that this awful state of affairs is actually as you think?"

"Unfortunately, no," replied Fairbanks. "If I had do you suppose I would remain silent? No; I would risk scorn, contempt, and disbelief, and would proclaim my conviction from the house-tops. But I have none. I only know that I *know* there is trouble, bad trouble, in the wind, and further than that I cannot say."

Chaloner sat silent for a few seconds, stricken dumb by his chum's strange words and manner; then he remarked! "But you *must* have *some* grounds of some sort for your belief, man; a fellow does not become convinced that an army is about to rise in revolt without some——"

"I was talking over the 'wire' to-day—and have been for some time past—with a friend of mine in Delhi, and he is of the same opinion as myself," interrupted Fairbanks; "and at Delhi, too, it is possible for the initiated to foresee what is coming. You know what a *chuppati* is, I suppose?" he enquired, somewhat irrelevantly Chaloner thought.

"Why, yes," was the reply; "a sort of cake, isn't it?"

"Well, something of the sort," said his friend. "Now those cakes, *bearing a message of some kind not comprehended by Europeans*, have lately been passed from hand to hand throughout all India; they have been seen north, south, east, and west, and there is no doubt that they are a signal. It is not known how they pass, or who passes them, but pass they do; and the sign is evil. Every cataclysm in Indian history has been preceded by the passage from hand to hand of these *chuppatis*. Does it not seem to point, then, to such a cataclysm being almost upon us now? That, Peter, is only one out of hundreds of significant incidents that I could mention, and the wonder to me is, not so much how it is that people cannot see and read, but how it is that they can *avoid* seeing and comprehending what seems to some of us to be so plain. Oh, those generals, colonels, and officers commanding of yours! *How* can they be so blind, after so long a residence in India as theirs has been?"

"But, Neville," broke in Chaloner, "if you really believe all this, it is surely your duty to warn the authorities, never minding what they may think of you; then your part, at least, will have been done; and if they will not heed——"

"No use, Chaloner, I tell you, no use," replied Fairbanks despondently. "I repeat, I have no proof. Can I go to a man and say: 'Have you not noticed the significance of the *chuppatis* now passing from hand to hand?' Certainly not. He would deem me mad. But we will speak of this later, old man; we had better drop it now, for here we are at 'Old Brown Bess's husband's'" (the name among the British soldiery by which General Hewlitt was known).

"All right!" said Chaloner, as the dog-cart came to a halt. "I'll see you later, somewhere. Don't forget that I want you to come and sleep at my place to-night."

"Thanks, I will," replied Fairbanks, and, the two young men getting down, the horse and dog-cart were led away by a white-coated *khidmutgar* to the stabling reserved for the guests' vehicles. Chaloner and Fairbanks entered the brilliantly-lighted house, and were presently in the throes of greeting and introduction which preceded the commencement of the actual dancing; and it was some hours later before they met again in the refreshment-room, collars and cuffs limp with perspiration, and themselves feeling as though they had just emerged from a Turkish bath.

"Well, how are you enjoying yourself?" asked Fairbanks, as the two young men flung themselves on to a couch in the ante-room and proceeded to mop their glistening faces.

"First rate," replied Chaloner merrily. "I always appreciate the General's 'hops'; but, I say, I'm most confoundedly hungry and thirsty, for I had very little time for dinner this evening—too busy getting ready for this," waving his hand toward the ball-room which they had just left. "Can't we get a snack to eat? I suppose it's not too early?"

"Too early? why, no," replied Fairbanks. "Look, there's the *khansaman* behind the buffet now, getting ready to serve out. Come along, and we'll hold him up for a bite to eat, and a good, long claret cup. Hi! *khansaman-ji*," he continued, dragging his not unwilling friend up to the buffet, "what have you got there, eh? Give us something to eat and drink, and *jeldi* (hurry); we are starving, my friend and I."

The *khansaman*, who knew both lads well, grinned, and handed them the required refreshments, which they proceeded to consume without leaving the buffet, their eyes roving round the room meanwhile, taking in the splendid decorations of the apartment and the rich skins and furnishings with which it was supplied. Suddenly Fairbanks uttered a suppressed cry, and strode across the room toward the sofa upon which they had, a short time previously, been seated. Something had attracted the young man's attention, something which lay upon the floor, and which was just visible at the very edge of the shadow cast by the sofa. Quickly he stooped down, thrust his arm under the couch, grasped and withdrew the article which he had seen, and thrust it surreptitiously into his pocket. Then he strolled back to his friend, at the same time keenly watching the white-clad *khansaman*, whose efforts to appear unconscious of the incident would have been amusing had the whole situation not been so serious. Presently the man could endure young Fairbanks's scrutiny no longer, and, with a muttered excuse, left the refreshment-room on the pretext of fetching something from the kitchen. Fairbanks watched him go, with a wry smile on his lips.

"What is it? What did you find?" whispered Chaloner as soon as the butler had disappeared.

"What I expected," replied Fairbanks solemnly, drawing his hand from his pocket and holding it out, open, toward his friend.

"Why, that's one of those *chuppatis* you were talking about surely, isn't it?" asked Chaloner, turning the piece of unleavened bread over and over in his hands.

"It is," answered Fairbanks, "and it means, unless I am much mistaken, that trouble is nearer than even I supposed. It may mean that this very night——! Oh, Peter, Peter, if I could only make others see and understand what I can see so plainly! But if I told them what this means, they'd merely pronounce me mad—and do nothing. I feel as though the safety of this whole station lies upon my shoulders, and yet the power to save it lies not with me but with those who *will not* be convinced. If I could but get some proof! Look here, Peter," he went on feverishly, "I can't remain here watching those fools dancing on the very edge of eternity. I shall get my cloak, run over to the telegraph *cutcherri* (office), and see whether I can get any further information."

"I'll come with you," exclaimed Chaloner, now beginning in some measure to comprehend and share his friend's alarm. "But I forgot to tell you before that Urghab Ali said to-night: 'If trouble comes, warn your friend not to go near the telegraph office.' He said that would be the first place 'they' would make for."

"Aye, so it would," agreed Fairbanks. "But I should try to get there first, all the same. Now, if you're ready, we'll get our cloaks and start. Perhaps no one will be awake at the other end of the line; but we shall see. Let's leave the dog-cart and walk; if we don't come back we can easily send over for it."

The two young men slipped unobtrusively out of the house, and were presently striding along the road toward the telegraph office. Curiously enough, although they met very few people, the whole town of Mirapur seemed on this particular night to be full of a dull, subdued murmur, as though the whole population were whispering in unison. There was something almost unnerving as well as sinister about the murmur too; it resembled the very distant roar of a fanatic mob, thirsting for blood, and Chaloner could not repress a shudder of apprehension and foreboding as the fancy struck him.

"I feel like that too," remarked Fairbanks, who had

observed the shiver, "and you may be quite sure that there's good reason for it! Hallo! who the dickens is this?"

"This" resolved itself into the gigantic form of a native cavalry officer, *subâhdar* of Chaloner's own regiment, one Shere Singh, a man of unblemished character and unswerving loyalty. He loomed up out of the shadows as though he had been waiting for the two Englishmen, and, standing square in their path, saluted.

"*Salaam*, sahibs!" he exclaimed.

"*Salaam aleikûm*, Shere Singh!" returned Chaloner. "Dost wish to speak with me? If so, say on."

"I do," replied the man in his deep, rumbling bass. "I was coming to speak to thee at the house of the General; but, since I have met thee here, so much the better. Sahib, trust not the men of the Fifth, nor the men of the other two regiments. There is trouble brewing. What it is I know not, for they speak not in my hearing, knowing me for a loyal man; but mischief of some sort they certainly mean, and I considered it my duty to warn thee. Go armed from now on, trust no man, walk not alone by night, and lock thy doors. To thee also, Fairbanks Sahib, I say beware. Let all the *Farângis* beware, lest they be utterly cut off. Nay, seek not to stay me, sahibs; spies are everywhere, and if they suspect me of warning you I am a dead man. One thing more, ere I go; I have this night learnt that the Rajah of Bithûr, him they call the Nana Sahib, is not the friend of the *Farângis* he pretends to be, but their deadly enemy! He it is who sits, like a spider in its hole, weaving a web that will enmesh the whole British *Râj*, unless ye take care! Farewell, sahibs; betray me not!" And the silent-footed *subâhdar* vanished in the darkness.

"Phew!" whistled Fairbanks, as they resumed their walk; "Nana Sahib, eh! That's news indeed. Why, everybody believes the fellow to be a very pillar of loyalty and strength. He is, to all appearance, an educated, cultivated gentleman, friendly to us to a degree. He has lived in England, knows our ways, and is said to be more English than we are ourselves."

"Yes," replied Chaloner. "I know the man personally, and so do my people. Indeed, he stayed at my father's house for some time when he was in England. He parted from us in a bit of a huff, though, for he happened to take a great fancy to my sister Kate, and pestered her to such a degree with his unwelcome attentions that the guv'nor had politely to request him to terminate his visit. The beggar went; but he managed, much to our annoyance, to steal a locket containing a miniature portrait of Kate, and, for aught I know, has it now. I didn't care much for him myself, but surely—*surely* he would not turn against the people who showed him so much kindness in the old country? He was fêted and honoured wherever he went, and everyone gave him the best time possible."

"That's so," agreed Fairbanks; "but you never can tell what these natives will do. They may wear the mask of friendship for years, in order to gain their ends, and then, when the time comes, they drop the mask and exhibit the cruelty and cunning of fiends incarnate. Hearing what you have just told me, I am glad that your sister is safe at home in England; for when once a man like the Nana sets his mind on a thing, he usually does not rest until he has obtained his desire. Here we are, however, at the office. Come inside and I'll see whether I can get hold of the Delhi operator. He may have some news."

Once inside, and the keyboard illuminated by a small oil-lantern—for they did not wish their presence to be detected if that could be avoided—Fairbanks began to tap out the call for the man at Delhi. For some minutes he called in vain, and then, "*click, click, click*", came the answer, enquiring who was there.

Fairbanks informed him, and then put his own questions.

The reply came rapidly, but in quick, hurried jerks, as though the operator were labouring under great excitement. Chaloner, watching his friend, saw Fairbanks's mouth set in a hard, stern line; and presently, when the message had ceased, the young clerk turned to him and said solemnly: "It sounds pretty bad, my boy. Davidson reports that the sepoys in Delhi have evidently had news of some kind, for they are all frightfully excited. Several Europeans have been insulted in the streets, and one or two bungalows have been burned; but so far nobody has been killed, fortunately. What makes matters so serious, though, is the fact that there are scarcely any British soldiers there, while there are any number of native regiments. There are only a few score white troops in the city, while the sepoys are numbered by thousands. Well, we can do no more to-night, so what do you say to going home? I don't feel much inclined for any more dancing; do you?"

"No," answered Chaloner, "I do not. Let's go home, by all means." And together the two young men made their way through the silent, moonlit streets toward the quarter of the city where Chaloner's bungalow was situated, meeting singularly few people on the road, which was usually well filled even at this late hour in the evening. But both lads were too fully occupied with their own dismal thoughts to pay much attention to this circumstance, and the house on the Delhi road was reached with scarcely more than a score of words exchanged between them.

They entered the house through the back veranda, in order to summon the Pathan from the servants' quarters to go and bring back the dog-cart and horse which had been left at General Hewlitt's; and Urghab Ali having at length been aroused from a sound slumber, and made to understand what was required, Chaloner and Fairbanks went into the house, lighted the lamp in Chaloner's little sitting-room, and sat down to a quiet chat and smoke before finally turning in for the night.

They had been conversing in low tones upon the matter uppermost in their minds, for about a quarter of an hour, when both lads were startled to hear the sound of a sneeze and a snort from the direction of the front veranda.

Chaloner's hand flew instinctively to the place where his sword usually swung; but an instant later he realized the meaning of the sound.

His dog Rough, a big Rampur hound, was in the habit of sleeping on the door-mat during the warm weather, and the animal had evidently just been awakened by a mosquito, or some similar insect, settling on his nose.

"Here, Rough, Rough!" he called, and presently the great dog was heard lazily padding his way along the dark passage towards the sitting-room.

As he entered, Fairbanks called the animal to him, for, like his friend, he was exceedingly fond of dogs. Rough obeyed and placed his splendid head on Fairbanks's knee, looking up into the lad's eyes, and then Fairbanks saw that there was something in the dog's mouth.

"Hallo! what have you got there, you sinner?" he asked. "Drop it, sir; drop it at once!" And with an apologetic look the hound dropped the object upon the floor at Fairbanks's feet.

The young man stooped, picked it up, and then looked long and meaningly at his friend.

What Rough had picked up on the front veranda, and what Fairbanks now held in the palm of his open hand, was another of those mysterious *chuppatis*, about which they had both been talking earlier that same evening!

CHAPTER II

"To Delhi! To Delhi!"

It was the evening of the day following General Hewlitt's ball, the evening of that fateful Sunday, 10th May, 1857, and the sun was sinking into a sea of clouds, red as the blood of the Europeans who were so soon to fall beneath the merciless *tulwârs* of the rebel cavalry, and before the bullets of the mutinous sepoys.

The church bells were ringing sweetly on the evening air, the service having, for some reason best known to head-quarters, been advanced by half an hour on this particular occasion; and the soldiers and officers were getting themselves into their parade uniforms in order to attend the garrison church. It was rumoured, also, that there was to be a moonlight parade after service, at which General Wilmot, the officer commanding, would take the opportunity to address the troops. Whether this was true or not will never be known, nor will it ever be known what it was that the general intended to speak about, for the parade was never held, and the lips of the general himself were very soon to be closed by death; but at this particular moment everything was as quiet and peaceful as an English Sabbath evening, and there was absolutely nothing to warn men of what the next hour was to bring forth.

At last officers, white soldiers, civilian men, women, and children were all either just completing their preparations, or were on their way to the various places of worship; and among them were our friends Chaloner and Fairbanks, the former in full uniform, his sword swinging bravely from his hip, his white-and-gold turban cocked jauntily on his head, and his long, black cavalry boots shining from Urghab Ali's efforts until their wearer could almost have seen to shave in them. In his French-grey uniform, with the gold shoulder-straps and shining brass buttons, the young Englishman looked what he was all over, a clean, wholesome soldier of the Queen, and he carried himself as though he knew it.

His companion, who as usual had been to call for him, was dressed in cool white, from his broad *solah topi* (sun hat) to his neat canvas boots, and instead of a sword carried only a light walking-cane. The two lads were hurrying along as fast as the heat would allow, for they were a little late; and although Chaloner had no "church draft" to pick up—his regiment being, of course, all non-Christians—he did not like to go in after the service had commenced.

The dusty parade-ground was empty of all but themselves, everybody else having already gone forward, and Chaloner was on the point of suggesting that they should hasten their steps a little, when, from the direction of the native cavalry barracks where the Fifth Bengal Cavalry—Chaloner's own regiment—were quartered, came a dull, confused sound, as of the distant shouting of many voices, while at the same time a somewhat similar sound made itself heard away in the city itself, proceeding apparently from the quarter where the prison was situated.

"Hallo! hallo!" exclaimed Chaloner, halting; "what's that? It sounds as though some kind of row had broken out among those fellows of mine at the barracks. I wonder whether I ought to step across and see what is the matter, instead of going to church, or whether the *subâhdar*, Shere Singh, will be able to attend to the business, whatever it may be? I think, perhaps, I had better go myself. If there should be a shindy, they may pay attention to a white man where they would not obey one of their own kind. And what, I wonder, is the meaning of that row over there in the city?" he went on, as the distant sounds from that direction became more clearly audible. "I tell you what it is, Fairbanks, I don't like that sound overmuch; there is a tone in it that is wicked, and it's getting louder and nearer every second. See here, I think you'd better sprint back to my place, and stay there instead of going to church; for you're unarmed, and if there should by any chance be a riot in progress, you will be likely enough to be in the way, and perhaps get hurt. As for me, I'm off to the barracks. See you later."

"Here, stop a moment," protested Fairbanks, catching his excited friend's sleeve; "I'm not going to skulk in your house; don't you think it for a minute. On the contrary, I'm going to the telegraph office; for somehow it's in my mind that a message or two will need to be sent from here before we're much older. I shall stay there until the very last second, and then, if I can, I will make for your house. If I am at neither of those places you may conclude that it will be no use looking anywhere else, for I shall be dead. That row in the barracks and the other in the town mean the beginning of serious trouble, or I'm greatly mistaken. Now off you go, and God keep us all this night! But stay!" he added, as the two clasped hands. "Here comes one of the British infantry officers, running as if for his life too. There's something very wrong indeed, I'm afraid, Peter; for see, his face is streaming with blood, and he staggers as he runs. Here's news at last, and bad news too, with a vengeance. Let's hear what he has to say before we move."

At this moment the officer, who happened to be a friend of Chaloner's, dashed up, breathless, and almost exhausted with loss of blood. Even as he reached them he collapsed upon the ground, and several precious moments passed before he was able to speak.

Then: "The native cavalry have mutinied!" he gasped. "They have saddled up, gone to the prison, liberated the *sowârs* we imprisoned yesterday, and all the other prisoners, the thieves, *badmâshes*, and sweepings of the city, and are even now burning and slaying in the European quarter! The sepoys, too, have broken out of barracks and are helping their friends of the cavalry to burn, loot, and outrage. Hurry to the British cantonment; warn General Wilmot; request him to turn out the troops and form them up, fully armed, on the parade-ground, for those fiends of sepoys and *sowârs*'ll be here presently. They caught me, and I only just escaped with my life; and unless they can be checked at once the whole city will rise, when heaven only knows what'll happen. Run, man, run; never mind me; I'm done for, and I've kept you too long already."

And even as Chaloner turned and sprinted at full speed toward the British cantonments, while Fairbanks rushed away to the telegraph office, a cloud of dust at the other side of the parade-ground announced the arrival of the advance-guard of the rebel cavalry, and a red light, which was not that of the setting sun, slowly began to flicker and spread over the western quarter of the city, from which were already beginning to rise those cries of men and women in mortal agony which were soon to go ringing all through India. Chaloner saw, heard, and understood, and he ran as he had never run in his life before. The lives—aye, more than the mere lives—of his fellow Europeans hung, he believed, upon his fleetness of foot, and he had no time to spare for even a thought of pity for the unfortunate officer who still lay gasping in the dust, at the mercy of the keen swords of the Fifth Bengal Cavalry mutineers.

But he did wonder where Subâhdar Shere Singh was, native captain of the rebel *sowârs*. Surely *he* was not among that group of galloping horsemen whose *tulwârs* were flashing dully red in the fast-sinking evening sun! But, if not, where was he?

Straight as an arrow Chaloner sped to the British lines, and rushed breathlessly into the mess-room, where he knew those officers who had not gone to the *girja ghur* (church) would be most likely to be found at that hour; and a few seconds later was gasping out his awful news.

"General Wilmot and gentlemen," he exclaimed, "if the lives of the Europeans at Mirapur are to be saved to-night, I beg you to call out the British troops at once! The native infantry and the Fifth Cavalry have risen and are already burning and slaying all over the city. They have liberated the prisoners, and the *badmâshes* are committing nameless crimes. This is true, for a wounded British officer lies on the parade-ground, even now, to prove my words."

Wilmot, a stout, heavy man of about sixty years of age, red of face, with a hobnailed liver, and temper to match, was, unfortunately, one of a class of officer of which India was far too full at that time. A system of promotion by seniority, instead of by capability, had produced a type of officer utterly unsuited to Indian requirements. These men were wrapped up in their own selfishness and conceit; they had no idea of how to conduct a campaign; drank heavily; idled away their days instead of attending to their work; transferred their own duties to the shoulders of their subordinates; and were obsessed by a most implicit confidence in the loyalty of the native troops, a confidence which in certain cases remained unshaken—impossible as it may seem—in despite of indubitable proof to the contrary produced before their very eyes!

Such a man was Brigadier Hewlitt, Officer Commanding the district, and such another was General Wilmot, Officer Commanding the British troops at Mirapur. He allowed Chaloner to finish his impassioned appeal, and then, turning to his brother officers, remarked coolly: "Our young friend seems a little excited, gentlemen, and apparently forgets that courtesy of manner which is due to his seniors. Mr. Chaloner," addressing Peter, "I cannot but think that your very obvious state of excitement has led you to exaggerate what is, no doubt, nothing more than a passing disturbance in the city, which, perhaps, our loyal native troops have taken it upon themselves to quell, thus leading you and the other officer to believe that the sepoys have joined hands with the rioters. That is, of course, absurd; that is a course of action which *my* men—" with a pronounced accent on the "my"—"would never adopt. You say that Europeans are in danger from the rioters. Well, I am satisfied that the native troops are quite competent to put down the disturbance without the necessity of calling upon our countrymen to assist them. You evidently believe what you have heard, sir, and therefore I will excuse——"

"But, sir," interrupted Chaloner hotly, aghast that the man could not actually *feel* the tension in the air, and angry that he should waste precious moments in fatuous rigmarole, "I am not relating what I have *heard*, but what I have myself actually *seen*! I have seen and spoken with the man who was wounded; I have seen the flames of the burning houses; and I have seen my own men riding back from freeing the prisoners! Oh, sir, I beg of you to act. Every minute lost now means the loss of precious lives."

"You say you have actually *seen* this?" queried Wilmot lazily, with incredulity still in the tones of his voice. "Perhaps, then, we had better stroll down and see for ourselves what the matter really is. I am certain it is nothing more than a little temporary excitement, possibly the result of too much *bhang* (hashish), and assuredly is not an occasion for calling out British troops. Come, gentlemen, take your swords and we will go down. Mr. Chaloner, I hope you will be able to justify the trouble to which you are putting us, for it is a serious matter to disturb your superiors without due cause."

"I assure you, sir, that you will find ample justification," answered Chaloner; "but, if I may be permitted to say so, I do not think you are wise to go without an escort. The native troops are simply blood-mad, and——"

"That is quite sufficient, sir," interrupted Wilmot sternly; "I will not hear another word against the men. Captain Jones," turning to one of the red-coated officers, "have the goodness to summon the bugler. Now that I am, against my better judgment, going to look into this, I will parade the men, and show how little truth there is in Mr. Chaloner's supposition."

Chaloner flushed hotly under the innuendo, but held his peace. The more talk the slower Wilmot would be; so he merely followed the dignified procession down the barrack steps, controlling his eager haste as best he might.

As they gained the open, however, a dreadful scream echoed from the parade-ground, causing more than one gallant cheek to turn pale, and the red glare of burning houses became immediate and convincing proof of the truth of Chaloner's words.

"By Jove, there seems to be more trouble than I imagined!" exclaimed Wilmot, tugging at his moustache. "Mr. Chaloner, I beg your pardon. You did right to inform me of this. Come along, gentlemen, we must look into this at once." And he started to run ponderously in the direction of the cry, drawing his sword as he ran, while upon the evening air there rose savage shouts, now plainly perceptible, of: "*Deen! Deen! Fâtteh ki bhai!*" (The Faith! the Faith! Victory to the brotherhood!) mingled with shrieks of despair, and other cries of: "Death to the *Farângis!* Down with the sahibs! Burn, brothers; burn and slay! burn and slay! *Deen! Deen!*"

The sound was truly awful; there could no longer be any doubt that a very serious revolt was in progress, and that, notwithstanding Wilmot's conviction to the contrary, the native troops were indeed engaged in the work of slaughter. Only armed soldiers could be responsible for those fearful cries, since the liberated *badmâshes* would not yet have had time to provide themselves with weapons. Besides, as the English officers approached the parade-ground, the clatter of horses' hoofs and the ring of steel on steel became plainly audible, likewise the deep-toned hum of martial voices, cheering on the slayers.

A few seconds later the little group reached the parade-ground at a run, and Wilmot almost stumbled over the corpse of the young officer who had brought the awful news to Chaloner. But now the body was cut and slashed almost beyond recognition. The native cavalry had passed that way, and their sabres had done the cruel work.

As soon as Wilmot could find breath he almost shrieked to the bugler: "Sound the assembly, boy; sound the assembly! By heavens! those who have done this deed shall pay dearly."

The poor man's world of dreams was tumbling about his ears, and a very few more surprises of this sort would suffice to throw him off his balance completely. As yet he could scarcely believe his own eyes.

As the clear, silvery notes of the "Assembly" shrilled across the open space, the massed body of native infantry and cavalry at the far end of the ground appeared to shiver slightly, and instinctively gathered itself into some kind of military formation. The habit of discipline was not to be discarded in a second, and by the time that the General and his staff had reached the scene the troops were standing in something like order, the two infantry regiments drawn up in two long columns, four deep, and the *sowârs*, their swords still drawn, formed up in line, two deep.

Wilmot raised his right hand, and a silence as of death fell upon the square as he began to address them in the vernacular.

Calling them "brothers", and appealing to their loyalty, he pleaded with them to return to their barracks, promising that, if they did so, any excesses they might have commited "in their excitement" would be forgiven them. He also called for one company of the Fifty-ninth regiment to stand out, and to prepare to follow him, for the purpose of hunting down and taking back to jail the prisoners who had "broken out".

But not a man among them moved in response to his impassioned appeal, not a single gleam of compunction appeared in the fierce eyes of any one of them. One and all stared right in front of them, over the heads of the British officers, and more than a few were already beginning to finger the locks of their muskets in a very suggestive manner.

The air was charged with electricity. One unconsidered movement, one injudicious word, one slip, however small, and the little band of Englishmen would be shot down, cut to pieces, and ridden over, before they had time to breathe a prayer. Yet not one of them blinked an eyelid, not a hand crept to sword-hilt, not a man showed even a trace of fear, near though death was; and presently the ranks subsided into immobility again. The crisis passed.

Then shouted Wilmot: "Once more, men, I appeal to you, for the last time. Stand forth all those who are on the side of the British *Râj*. Where are the loyal men? Where is the Subâhdar Shere Singh? Surely he is not our enemy. I say, who is on our side? Let the true men stand forth!"

Still not a movement.

Chaloner, raging with shame at the defalcation of his own *sowârs*, looked for Shere Singh. If he could see and speak to him, perhaps the tall Sikh might influence his comrades; but Shere Singh was not there. Loyal or disloyal, the man was not present, had not been present, he knew, from the first. Where on earth could he be?

Then the bolt fell.

Wilmot, enraged at the total lack of response, stepped up to one man who was regarding him with a more insolent stare than the rest, and, grasping him by the collar, dragged him out of the ranks and hurled him savagely to the ground.

"Thus will I treat ye all, ye *sûri ki butchai*! (sons of pigs)," he shouted, glaring at the sepoys with eyes suffused with tears of rage. But he spoke no other word, he never lifted a finger to any other man.

A little ripple of movement shivered along the line of men, the muskets rose to the charge, then to the present, and the Englishmen looked Death in the face without flinching.

Only one weapon spoke; there was a flash of flame, a puff of smoke, not from the ranks, but from the rifle of the man Wilmot had handled, and without a cry the General fell to the ground, dead, the second British soldier to give his life among the thousands who fell during the course of the great Indian Mutiny.

For a second the lives of all hung in the balance, and then Chaloner stepped up to his *sowârs*. The sudden movement released the tension, and the muskets were again grounded; but nothing that the young man could say could bring one answering gleam to the eyes of the cavalrymen. They had set their hands to the plough and would not be turned back.

Then a voice rang out fiercely: "Brothers, to Delhi! to Delhi! The British *sirkar* (Government) is dead; it is we who have done the deed. The King, the Great Mogul, shall reign again in Delhi; and the *Farângis* shall be driven into the sea, the black water, from whence they came. Delay no longer, brothers; our friends await us there; so to Delhi, I say, to Delhi!"

The appeal did not go unanswered.

High in air were tossed caps and turbans; bayoneted muskets were thrust upward, to the accompaniment of a wild shout; among the ranks of the cavalry, swords flickered and clashed as the men brandished them above their heads, while illuminating the whole weird scene there shone the red, leaping flames of the burning bungalows, the finishing touch of horror being given by the shouts of the ravaging *badmâshes*, and, worse still, the shrill screams of the wounded and dying.

Came a short, sharp order, and the *sowârs* wheeled upon their own right files and galloped away toward the south, shouting: "To Delhi! To Delhi!" at the full pitch of their lungs. They made no attempt to molest the astounded group of Englishmen, but passed them by for higher game—the loot of the ancient capital. So, too, the sepoys. Not a hand was raised against the whites, but, opening their ranks to avoid them, the two long lines of men swept forward, reiterating the shout of: "To Delhi! To Delhi!" and the group of officers was left behind, man gazing into the eyes of man, comrade gripping the hand of comrade, asking wordlessly what was this fearful thing that had come to pass, and where and how would it all end?

For minutes they stood thus, as though all power of movement had left them; then their eyes fell upon the silent form of General Wilmot, from under whose red tunic a still redder stream was beginning to trickle, making a sinister-looking pool in the dust beside the dead figure, and the spell was broken.

As though suddenly galvanized into life, four men dashed forward and seized each an arm or a leg, while two more supported the body in the middle; and thus, led by Chaloner, the little group made their way back to the barracks, at the best speed of which they were capable. They had one thought only—the determination to wreak vengeance upon the men who had been untrue to their salt, who had already slain two British officers and no one as yet knew how many more of their countrymen—and countrywomen, and who were already on their way to Delhi to consummate their triumph and slay as many more Europeans as they could lay hands upon.

Those men must be pursued and overtaken before they could reach Delhi, that was certain, or there was no knowing what atrocities might be committed there among the all but defenceless population. The few score British soldiers would stand no chance at all against the multitude of sepoys, especially when their triumphant comrades arrived, all flushed from their successful revolt at Mirapur.

Successful it certainly had been, principally because the dead Wilmot had not been able to bring himself to realize the possibility that his sepoys could turn disloyal. Had he but believed the news that Chaloner had brought, at once called out the British troops, and marched them to the parade-ground, the native soldiery might easily have been overawed and disarmed, and the mutiny would have been quelled ere it had had time properly to raise its head.

Even now it was not altogether too late to repair the error. If the British cavalry, with a battery or two of flying artillery, were at once dispatched in pursuit, the enemy might be overtaken and crushed before he could reach the safety of Delhi. Had anyone yet telegraphed the news to that city, that mutineer soldiers were on the way, and warning the English there to close the gates and hold out until the pursuing column could arrive?

Chaloner was able to answer this question by assuring the enquirer that his chum, Fairbanks, had gone to the office at the first alarm, and that there was no doubt the news had been flashed everywhere some time ago.

Then, accompanied by another officer, he made his way in all haste to Brigadier-General Hewlitt's quarters, to inform the old gentleman of what had occurred, and secure his permission for a flying column to be sent in immediate pursuit.

It seemed almost an impossibility that any Englishman in Mirapur could still be unaware of the tragedy that had been, and was still, taking place in the city; but so it proved to be. Chaloner and his companion, a lieutenant of the Seventy-third regiment, were informed, upon their arrival, that General Hewlitt was asleep, and had left orders that he was not to be disturbed under any circumstances; and so stubborn was the servant that, finally, Chaloner lost his temper, flung the fellow down the steps, and entered the house with the lieutenant, intending to do his own announcing.

But Hewlitt had, as it happened, been awake, and, hearing the disturbance, was proceeding angrily to the door himself when he cannoned into Chaloner in the dimly-lighted passage.

"Hallo! who the—what—who are you, sir?" he shouted angrily. "What do you mean by coming here and raising this disturbance? Did not the *khidmutgar* tell you that I was not at home to anybody?"

"Yes, sir, he did—or at least he tried to do so. It is not the man's fault," answered Chaloner quickly, while the lieutenant of the Seventy-third placed himself at his companion's elbow, as though affording him moral support against the General's wrath.

"But," continued the irregular horseman, "my errand would not admit of delay, sir, and I was obliged to act as I have done. I have awful news to communicate, sir. The whole of the native regiments have mutinied; they have broken open the jail, liberated the prisoners, burnt European bungalows, have murdered two British officers, and, finally, have started for Delhi, where they intend to repeat the process. I have been sent by my brother officers, sir, to ask you to take action at once, and to give orders that a flying column of British troops shall be dispatched in pursuit, so that the mutineers may be brought to book before they can reach the shelter of Delhi."

"What! What's this? What's all this farrago of nonsense, Mr. Chaloner? Surely, sir, you must be intoxicated! My sepoys would never dream of acting in the way you have described."

"Yet the fact remains, sir, that they *have*," replied Chaloner hotly, "and the bodies of the murdered officers are there to prove it. If more proof is needed, you have but to glance out of the windows at the back of this house and you will see the glow of flames from the burning bungalows, will hear the cries of the Europeans who are, even while I speak, falling beneath the daggers of the bazar rabble and *badmâshes*."

"Dear me! dear me!" stuttered Hewlitt, convinced at last that Chaloner was sober and speaking the truth; "you don't say so? This is indeed very dreadful. Dear, dear! very terrible. But, really, I do not see what I can do to mend matters. The sepoys have got away, you say, therefore the danger to us is over, I presume. Better let well alone, and not interfere with them; they will come back when they have finished their spree—for that, I feel sure, is all it is—and will feel ashamed of their momentary lapse from discipline. I wish you good evening, gentlemen."

For a few seconds the two young men stood aghast, rooted to the spot at this exhibition of senile indecision and lack of initiative; then the man of the Seventy-third fairly thundered: "You do not see what to do, sir? Why, think of what will happen to our countrymen in Delhi if the mutineers are not overtaken before they get there! I am only a junior, General Hewlitt, but I can tell you what to do. Send a British flying column of cavalry and artillery after the scoundrels; that is the proper thing to do!"

"Sir, I think you forget to whom you speak," retorted Hewlitt feebly. "*I* give orders here; and my orders are that the men who are here remain. I cannot afford to send troops away on such a wild-goose chase as you suggest. I have not enough men. To send away such a column would leave me—Mirapur, I should say—defenceless almost; and that is a thing I will not do; no, not for ten Delhis! And now, I must ask you please to go; these unpleasant episodes are very distasteful to me, and I would rather hear no more. No, I do not wish to see Wilmot's body, poor fellow, nor to interview the other officers. You can take them my message, and it is that not a single

European soldier is to leave Mirapur without my written order."

Silently, almost as though stunned, the two young officers returned to the cantonment and reported their interview with Hewlitt. Their hearers were dumbfounded, overwhelmed, speechless with horror and rage. But what could they do against organized authority? To disobey the Brigadier would be rank mutiny, for which every one of them would be "broken". Had Wilmot lived he might have bearded the lion again, and wrung from him a consent of some sort; but nobody but Wilmot could do so, and Wilmot lay dead. No, there was nothing for it but obedience.

The Colonel, however, a man named Barnes, did not intend to take Hewlitt's orders too literally. He might not move men out of Mirapur, but there was plenty of work for keen swords and avenging arms in the city itself, where the bazar habitués still carried on their dreadful work. So without more ado Barnes himself led a couple of companies through the streets, clearing the rabble from their path and scattering them like chaff, quenching fires, blowing up houses to check the flames, bringing in the wounded, and arranging shelter for the homeless.

Before he started, however, he went with Chaloner to the telegraph office, to make sure that the news had gone to Delhi, and there they found Fairbanks and Shere Singh, the Subâhdar, who had met the young telegraphist and defended the office door while the lad tried to send his messages.

"Tried," because it was soon found that the lines had been cut, and that Mirapur was entirely isolated from communication with every other city. The mutineers had laid their plans well. Fairbanks had been all this time striving to establish communication, without success; and he and Shere Singh were on the point of abandoning the post when Barnes and Chaloner arrived.

"Well," said Barnes, as soon as he learned the news, "there is no use in wasting time trying to find the place where the wire is cut; it may be anywhere between here and Delhi. But Delhi must be warned somehow, and I shall call for volunteers immediately, to ride for the city and try to get there, by taking short cuts, in advance of the mutineers. I'll go now."

"No need, sir," interjected three voices, and Barnes, turning, saw three hands at the salute—Chaloner's, Fairbanks's, and Shere Singh's!

"How no need?" demanded Barnes. "Do you three mean——?"

"That we'll go; yes, sir," replied the trio. "We two whites," went on Chaloner, " will dye our faces and disguise ourselves; the Subâhdar here needs no disguise. We ride well; we all have our horses ready and can be away in half an hour. Let us go, sir."

Despite the seriousness of the situation Barnes could scarcely restrain a smile at the eager expression on the faces of the three; they were very much in earnest.

"All right!" he said presently, "go, and God be with you. But, remember, I am relying on you *to get through*, and unless you are quite sure of yourselves you had better let me send someone else."

"We are sure, sir," again came the voices in chorus, and with a final salute, and a curt "Very good!" Barnes strode away, to begin his work of policing the city, while the three volunteers started off for Chaloner's house to secure disguises, and to prepare for their hazardous ride.

Presently, the Subâhdar, who was mounted upon his great black stallion, Kala Nag (Black Snake), went off, at Fairbanks's request, to fetch that young man's horse, while the two friends continued their hurried walk.

"I can understand Shere Singh volunteering, but I'm hanged if I know why you want to come," laughed Chaloner presently to Fairbanks.

"Aha!" replied the latter; "you think, my military friend, that you and your pals are the only people who count in a thing of this sort. Well, maybe I'll be able to show you, a little later, that even a despised telegraph clerk has his uses, sometimes."

CHAPTER III

The Midnight Ride

ALTHOUGH it seemed to Chaloner as though the events of days had been crowded into the space of time which had elapsed since the wounded officer brought his dreadful news, as a matter of fact only one brief hour had passed, and the dust raised by the departed mutineers marching to Delhi had as yet barely settled back again on the road after the passage of their rear-guard.

Even now, ever and anon, rising shrill upon the still night air, could be heard the shrieks of the bazar murderers, and the shouts of the British soldiery as their avenging bayonets cleared the rabble from the streets. Already the work of retribution had begun, and had the gallant Colonel Barnes but been allowed to have his own way, the mutiny might have been nipped in the bud that very night, and the soil of India remained unstained by the blood of British women and children. If the senile Hewlitt could but have foreseen the results of his vacillation he might have summoned up sufficient energy and initiative to deal promptly and effectively with the situation; but, unhappily, there are none so blind as those who will not see, and the hour of destiny was allowed to pass unchallenged.

Meanwhile, once inside the bungalow, the two lads found ample proof that the house had received more than one visit from the mutineers who had been obliged to pass the place on their way to Delhi. The sepoys had doubtless expected to find therein something worth looting, and, being disappointed in that expectation, had, after the manner of their class, vented their anger upon those inanimate objects contained therein which were too large to take away, or not worth the trouble of removing.

What little furniture Chaloner possessed was hacked and splintered by sword-cuts, even the very cushions had been slashed to ribbons, while in one corner of the sitting-room the mutineers had collected a pile of combustibles and lighted it, in the hope of destroying the house. But, fortunately, they must have been too hurried to make a good job of it, and the heap had smouldered out without doing any further damage. His dog, Rough, was nowhere to be seen, and the young man guessed that he had attacked the intruders and had been slain for his pains.

Observing the state of affairs, Chaloner called anxiously for Urghab Ali—for he knew that the Pathan would have strenuously resisted the desecration of his master's house—and when he received no answer to his repeated summons he began to fear the worst. His fears were quickly justified, for, on entering his bedroom, with Fairbanks hard on his heels, he fell over something lying just beyond the door, and the light of the lantern at once revealed the body of the faithful Yusufzai, slashed and hacked almost out of recognition. The brave old man had been true to his salt, and had died at his post, as did so many native servants during those first dark days of the Mutiny.

With a sob in his throat, for he had become much attached to Urghab Ali, Chaloner tore down a curtain and threw it over the stiffening body, afterwards placing the sinister-looking object on a couch. These were all the funeral obsequies the Englishman could afford to give, since there was no time to dig a grave and bury the body decently if Delhi was to be saved. The lives of the people there were of more importance than many dead Pathans, and Chaloner immediately set about the business of disguising himself and Fairbanks as natives, without which disguise it would be madness to expect to reach Delhi unchallenged.

Fortunately, a short time previously, the officers had given a theatrical performance in aid of the Mirapur Hospital, and Chaloner had taken the part of a native servant, necessitating the dyeing of his face and hands. For this purpose he had obtained a quantity of a certain native preparation from the bazar, and there was still plenty of it left over to colour the entire bodies of each of the lads.

This, for safety's sake, they proceeded to do, being aware how easily discovery might happen if only hands and face were treated; and so quickly did they work, and did the stuff dry, that in a quarter of an hour nobody would have guessed that they were other than natives of the country. Chaloner then slashed the facings from his uniform, so that he might pass for an ordinary trooper, and gave Fairbanks his second uniform, similarly treated, so that the pair would be taken anywhere for a couple of mutineer *sowârs*.

He then found Urghab Ali's sword, and buckled it round his friend's waist, and gave him one of a pair of pistols which the sepoys had overlooked in their hurried search, himself retaining the other; and the two lads were ready for their hazardous ride as soon as Shere Singh should have brought along Nancy, Fairbanks's grey mare. His own horse, Don, Chaloner had saddled and bridled while Fairbanks was getting into his borrowed uniform and putting the finishing touches to his disguise.

They did not, however, wait for the Subâhdar in front of the house, lest belated mutineers should pass, see them, and suspect their identity, but remained in Chaloner's garden, safely hidden among the fruit-trees, until Shere Singh's ringing shout of "Hi! Chaloner Sahib, Fairbanks Sahib, are you there?" and the clatter of two horses' hoofs on the road outside announced that the gallant and faithful native officer had arrived.

He, like Chaloner and Fairbanks, had cut the facings from his uniform, and in addition had substituted a heavy, keen-edged *tulwâr* for his service sword, so that there was nothing but a general resemblance to identify him with the Subâhdar of the Fifth Bengal Cavalry. Indeed, the three of them might now be easily mistaken even by the mutineers themselves, Chaloner hoped, for a party of rebel *sowârs*, intent on doing a little looting and murder on their own account, away from the main body.

"*Mere khidmutgar mur-gya* (My *khidmutgar* is slain), Subâhdar Sahib," remarked Chaloner sadly to Shere Singh, as he and Fairbanks mounted outside the bungalow.

"Urghab Ali dead?" repeated Shere Singh, who, being a Sikh, had been a great friend of the Pathan. "Then, by the head of the great Guru, I will have vengeance on his murderers! To slay that old man! The dogs; the sons of pigs; betrayers of their salt! I, Shere Singh, will take a heavy reckoning for that, Chaloner Sahib. Bear thou me witness that I will exact ten lives of those rebel bazar-born thieves for that of Urghab." And he drew his sword and kissed the hilt in token of the oath, which he more than kept during the months that followed. It was an ill day for some of the mutineers when the defenceless Pathan was slain.

"But come, sahibs," he continued, sheathing the weapon; "sorry as I am to hear of Urghab's death, we may not linger here. Every minute lost now may mean a British life lost in Delhi ere to-morrow's sun sets. Let us go. I know a short cut to the city by way of the jungle paths, by which I hope we may avoid the sepoys, who will, naturally, proceed by the road. It is the sahibs' will that I lead the way?"

"Lead on, Subâhdar Sahib," replied Chaloner briskly; "lead on; we follow." And the long night ride to Delhi commenced, under the brilliant light of an Indian May moon.

Along the Delhi road, for a matter of five miles, the three horsemen swept at top speed, in the rear of the mutineers, swords swaying against the horses' sides, curb chains jingling, and accoutrements rattling, each man revelling in the intoxication of the pace, until Shere Singh, a little in advance, suddenly threw up his hand, and reined Kala Nag sharply in.

"It is somewhere near here, sahibs," he said, "that we leave the road and take to the jungle. Cast thine eyes about thee and see if thou canst find a large baobab-tree, somewhere away on the left. The path passes by that."

Separating, the three men patrolled the road in both directions for a few minutes, during which each execrated the precious time lost, and then came a shout from Fairbanks, a hundred yards ahead, that he could see the baobab-tree, and that there appeared to be a narrow path, leading off the road, just opposite where he was standing, that would lead past the spot.

Putting spurs to their horses, Chaloner and the Subâhdar galloped up; and Shere Singh at once announced that the path found was the right one. They therefore left the road and plunged into the jungle, taking care, first of all, to look carefully up and down the highway, to make sure there was no one else near to observe their movements; and they were soon cantering rapidly along, in single file, with Shere Singh leading, making very good progress considering the nature of the ground and the necessity for keeping continually on guard against the danger of being swept from the saddle by some low, overhanging bough.

As long as he lives—for he is still alive, and a hearty man in spite of his age—Chaloner will never forget that night ride. The scenery through which they passed, lighted up by the glorious moon, was beautiful in the extreme; the air was clear and comparatively cool; and the speed at which they were travelling, the errand on which they were engaged, sent the blood tingling through the veins of all of them like a draught of champagne. Up hill and down dale, without drawing bridle, the strong, big-limbed horses carrying them as though they were mere featherweights, the trio clattered. Past jungles in the depths of which they could hear the snarl of the hungry tiger seeking his prey; across streams and rivers, some small and narrow enough to gallop through at full speed, others deep and broad enough to necessitate swimming, they went, never halting, never slackening speed, until, about two o'clock in the morning, on the banks of a small stream, they pulled up for a brief breathing-space, to let the horses rest and snatch a few mouthfuls of grass and water, and to stretch their own weary limbs. They had then, said Shere Singh, come about half-way, and four or five hours more should see them at the northern gate of

Delhi. The question, however, was, would they arrive in time, or would the rebel *sowârs*, with a start of a couple or more hours, get there first? They would not know until they came in sight of the city; and, the horses being a little rested, the three messengers wasted no more time, but mounted again and continued their perilous ride.

They had been riding as fast as was possible, cantering along the level and walking up the hills, for about an hour after they had halted on the bank of the river, and the first faint streaks of dawn were beginning to show in the sky to the east when, very faint and far away in front of them, they fancied they caught the sound of the explosion of a musket or pistol. The Subâhdar, riding in advance as usual, to show the way, immediately threw up his hand—the signal they had previously decided upon as a silent command to halt.

"You heard that, sahibs?" he whispered. "That was undoubtedly the discharge of a gun, and a carbine at that, or I never heard the Fifth fire theirs. Depend upon it, *Huzoors*, I am not the only man who knows this path. Some of the cavalry have undoubtedly sneaked off by this short cut, so as to get to Delhi first, and start plundering before their comrades can arrive. There is only one thing for us to do, heaven-born," addressing Chaloner, "and that is to ride cautiously forward, and, unless they outnumber us hopelessly, give them battle, and try to slay them all. If we find them too many for us to tackle openly, we will ride as close up behind them as we can, unobserved, and then make a charge, trusting to our rush and their surprise to get through untouched. Once past, we need hardly fear being overtaken; for our horses are very strong, and those ahead must have ridden almost as fast as we, to be where they are.

"But if it comes to making a dash, and any of us

should be wounded or unhorsed, under no circumstances whatever must the others or the survivor, as the case may be, stay behind, or try to effect a rescue. The safety of Delhi depends on our getting through, and we must be ready to sacrifice ourselves for that purpose. Therefore there must be no loitering or hesitation, but one clean dash for it; and those who get through must continue to ride for their lives; while supposing one, or two, of us should be unable to do so, we must take our chance, and give our lives in the attempt to prevent the mutineers from pursuing the survivor. That, I think, *Huzoors*, is our only plan. Do you agree to it?"

"It seems about the only thing we can do, Subâhdar Sahib," replied Chaloner, after a thoughtful pause, "and I only hope the scoundrels ahead of us are not in force; for, if they are, I see very little chance of any of us getting through. I suppose you can't think of a better idea, Neville, can you?" he asked, turning to Fairbanks.

"I'm afraid not," replied the latter, "unless Shere Singh here knows another by-path which we could take and so avoid them altogether."

"There is one, certainly, sahibs," said the Subâhdar; "but it is merely a jungle track. It would mean very slow progress, so that the mutineers would be certain to get in ahead of us; and we might easily lose our way in the bush. I fear the only thing left to us is to do as I suggested."

"Then so be it," decided Chaloner. "Forward is the word. Come along, and let us get the thing over, since there is no alternative."

So, with a sharp command to the horses, the three men cantered ahead once more, in the fast-gathering light of an Indian summer's day. The air was already losing the grateful coolness of the night, and the motion of the horses was fast throwing them all into profuse perspiration. Soon, too, the sun would be above the horizon, and then the real discomfort would begin, as anyone will realize who has ever been obliged to take horse exercise under an Indian sun.

Still, discomfort and possibility of sunstroke notwithstanding, it was necessary to push ahead. They had promised Colonel Barnes that one at all events of them should carry the news through to Delhi, and they each resolved to carry out their promise at all costs, or perish in the attempt.

Half a mile or so farther on, at a bend in the road, they galloped, before they could rein up, over the body of a splendid tigress, from whose carcass the breath had even yet not quite departed; and close beside her lay a dead horse, which, they could recognize, had belonged to the Fifth Cavalry. A few yards distant was to be seen the corpse of the rider, a trooper of the same regiment, lying face downward on the dusty ground, his sword, snapped short off at the hilt, beneath him. The three riders could easily reconstruct the tragedy, and realized that here before them lay the explanation of the shot which had put them on their guard a short time previously.

Evidently the tigress, maddened by hunger—for she was thin to the point of starvation—had sprung upon one of the troopers, torn him from his saddle, and, despite his efforts to defend himself, had flung him down and crushed his skull like an eggshell. Then, apparently, one of the fellow's comrades had drawn his carbine and shot the brute, this being the report they had heard. Lastly, the horse, being dreadfully clawed about the haunches, had been mercifully destroyed, one of the men having cut its throat with his sabre.

Shere Singh's only comment was one of satisfaction that, at any rate, the tigress had been instrumental in reducing the odds against them by one; but Chaloner

C 745

"AT A BEND IN THE ROAD THEY GALLOPED OVER THE BODY OF A SPLENDID TIGRESS"

and Fairbanks, being less accustomed to the sight of death, could not repress a shudder as their eyes fell upon the dark pool of blood which was welling sluggishly from beneath the man's shattered head.

There was no time to be lost, however, and, merely stopping to possess himself of the carbine, which still remained in its bucket on the dead horse, and the trooper's supply of ammunition, Shere Singh gave the word "Forward!" and on they dashed again in the rear of the mutineer cavalry party, the Subâhdar examining the carbine as he rode, to make sure that it was loaded. Finding that it was, the reckless native officer drew two more bullets from the *sowâr's* pouch and rammed them down on top of the old load, careless whether the weapon should burst, when fired, or not. He wanted to make that one discharge do as much damage as possible, and heeded not a whit the danger to himself in firing it. He also changed the priming, lest it should have been spoiled by the damp night air, and replaced the old percussion-cap with a new one.

They had been riding for what seemed quite a long time, and the jungle was already showing signs of thinning out, when, as they swung round a bend in the path, they perceived, in front of them, the party of whom they were in pursuit, and, to their great delight, discovered that there were only four men for them to deal with. Also, as the wind was blowing strongly in their faces, there was the possibility that, unless some of the *sowârs* chanced to look back, they might be able to get almost within striking distance before the mutineers became aware that they were being pursued. With a glance over his shoulder at the two young men, and a joyous nod of his head, Shere Singh loosened his *tulwâr* in its scabbard, looked to the lock of his carbine, and, pressing his spurs home into his horse's sides, dashed forward after the as yet unsuspecting troopers. Chaloner and Fairbanks, with a sudden curious catching of the breath, followed his example.

Nearer and nearer yet they approached, and still the laughing, chattering *sowârs* had no idea that death was so near them. The strong wind of early morning, blowing directly in their faces, with the thud of their horses' hoofs, prevented them hearing the hoof-beats of their pursuers'; and it was not until Shere Singh and his companions were within a hundred yards that the troopers caught the sound, turned in their saddles, and then pulled up their horses.

Another circumstance greatly in favour of the pursuers was the fact that, disguised as the three were, the mutineers had at first no suspicion that they were anything else than a small party of their own friends, who had, perhaps, been delayed, and had been making up for lost time by taking the short cut through the jungle. It was only when they caught sight of Shere Singh's fierce face glaring at them from between his horse's ears, and recognized him for their loyal Subâhdar, that they realized these were no friends of theirs, but bitter enemies, and avengers of the slain.

The three messengers were but twenty yards distant when from the rebel *sowârs* there rose a cry: "*Bismillah!* 'tis Shere Singh, the Subâhdar!" And four swords flashed from their scabbards as the mutineers spread themselves across the road.

"*Ai! Margalla lôg; Farângi-ji ki fâtteh!*" ("Aye! ye rascals; victory to the British!") yelled the Subâhdar, hoarse with excitement and eagerness to slay; and, tucking the butt of the carbine under his arm, he fired it, like a pistol, at the two *sowârs* who were nearest together, immediately dropping the weapon, and whipping out his *tulwâr* at the very last moment, when he was almost upon them.

Fortunately for Shere Singh, the treble-shotted carbine

had not burst, and the three balls had certainly justified the risk. One of the *sowârs* fell off his horse, shot through the stomach, and was kicked to death by the frightened animal, while one of the other two bullets brought down the second man's horse, pinning its rider by the leg, and allowing the Subâhdar a free passage through. One of the other troopers cut savagely at the flying horseman, but missed, and nearly overbalanced with the violence of his own blow. Before he could recover and guard himself, Chaloner's sword was through his throat, and he reeled backward over his horse's crupper and crashed to the ground, dead. Fairbanks's pistol, fired at point-blank range, took the fourth man fair in the centre of the chest, and the last impediment on the road to Delhi slid slowly from his animal's back and collapsed in a crumpled heap at the edge of the jungle, coughing blood at every breath. It would be merely a question of minutes before he followed his two companions along the valley of death; and the three messengers were through, and away on their adventurous ride once more.

But, strangely enough, in their exultation they never dreamed that the fourth man, he who had been brought down by his horse, was not dead also. Shere Singh had imagined that one of his carbine bullets had struck the fellow, and never gave him another thought. It was a mistake, however. The man was merely stunned by his fall on the hard road, and the messengers were hardly out of sight before the trooper recovered sufficiently to drag his leg from under his dead horse and stand, somewhat feebly it is true, on his feet.

Close at hand, too, were three uninjured horses; and, after a good long pull at his water canteen, the *sowâr*, still a little dazed, managed to climb upon the best of them, and set off again, slowly, upon his interrupted journey.

If Shere Singh could only have become aware of the fact, and all that hung upon it, it is very certain that the fierce Sikh would have ridden back and slain the man out of hand; but he unfortunately believed that they had left four dead bodies behind them, and it was with light hearts and thankful that they pressed forward to Delhi, telling themselves that one serious danger, at all events, had been safely overcome, and that, all being well, they would still arrive in time to save the city.

As soon as he himself was safely through, Shere Singh, in spite of his insistence that each should look after his own safety only, pulled up, prepared to turn back and assist his young companions should they find any difficulty with the two remaining *sowârs*; but they were by his side almost before he had turned his horse, and he laughed in his beard as he saw the manner in which the two lads dealt each with his opponent.

"*Shabash* (bravo), *Huzoors!*" cried the Subâhdar, as Chaloner and Fairbanks swept up alongside him; "we have started well. That is four of the Pandies we have accounted for already; and one that the tigress slew makes five. But, alas that I should have to rejoice at the death of my own men! Fools that they have been, to have allowed themselves to be led away by the windy, empty talk of *fakirs* and half-crazy *mullahs*! They will pay for their folly with blood and tears. Repining, however, is useless, sahibs, and our work is not yet finished. Forward again, for our lives, and for the lives of those in Delhi!"

He sheathed his *tulwâr*, and Chaloner did the same after wiping the blade on his horse's mane. Fairbanks made shift to recharge his empty pistol, and the three continued their ride at a gallop.

For some time past the jungle bordering the track

had been getting thinner and the path broader, and about half an hour after their encounter with the *sowârs* they emerged into the open altogether, and found themselves upon a *Bâr*, or sort of heath, covered with low shrubs and small trees; while away in the distance, to the south of them, shining like a jewel in the morning sun, could be made out the dome of Hasan's tomb, situated on the road from Delhi to Mirapur. Beyond that again, looking like a beautiful fairy city, could be seen the towers and gilded minarets of Delhi itself, lying perhaps ten miles away. Their goal was in sight at last!

And now, too, they were fast approaching the danger zone. Not three miles away, upon their right hand as they rode, lay the Delhi-Mirapur road, along which the rebels were travelling at their best speed; and, notwithstanding the short cut which the three had taken, the mutineers had had a long start. It was possible that the cavalry among them, at any rate, might still be in front of the trio, on the road; and if they were it would mean that the messengers would have to keep to the heath, and that matters would resolve themselves into a race between the cavalry on the road and themselves on the rough ground. There was also the constant danger that they might be sighted by some of the mutineer scouts, in which case their capture and death would be almost inevitable. As yet, however, the road was not visible, and would not be so for some time—not, in fact, until they approached very close to Hasan's tomb.

Acting under Shere Singh's guidance, therefore, they headed in that direction, keeping eyes and ears well open for the first signs of the enemy; and half a mile to the north of the tomb they discovered them. A party of cavalry were cantering rapidly along the road, in a dense cloud of dust, and, unfortunately, they were so far ahead that they must inevitably arrive at the tomb before Chaloner and his companions could possibly hope to reach it. To endeavour to enter the city, then, by way of the road, would be sheer folly; the mutineer cavalry would be certain to reach the gates first, since they were already some distance in advance, and, even if overtaken, were in too great force for three men to dream of attacking them.

When Shere Singh topped a slight rise, and observed this state of affairs, his face fell for a few seconds, and he looked apprehensively in the other direction, to see if other rebels were coming. But, except for the advance squadron already mentioned, nothing else was in sight, and the Sikh's countenance cleared.

"There is nothing for it, *Huzoors*," he said, "but to keep to the rough ground. The road is out of the question, as we should be trapped between those *sûrs* in front and those who are certain to be not far behind. But if we ride hard, and look well where we go, there is still a chance that we may reach the gates first. It will be by a very small margin, however, and we may have a fight before we get in."

"Never mind that, Subâhdar," exclaimed Chaloner, a little impatiently; "the important thing is to get there. If we have to fight, well—we must; but perhaps we may be able to avoid it if we're quick. Lead on, Subâhdar Sahib, at your best speed, and we'll follow."

Shere Singh uttered a short laugh, spurred his horse forward, and the grim race against time was resumed. By keeping to the *Bâr* they were sheltered from the road, and were thus reasonably safe from discovery; but their own view of the city was also hidden, since the heath was well below the level of the main road, except in parts where it rose slightly, and they had therefore to trust entirely to the Subâhdar's sense of direction.

Fortunately, this was excellent, and after an hour's hard riding Chaloner was overjoyed and surprised, on coming to a sudden rise, to perceive the Kashmir Gate but a short mile in front of them. A quick glance to the rear, however, showed that, although they had reached the road at a spot a little in advance of the mutineer cavalry, the latter were a bare couple of hundred yards behind; and he shouted the news to the Subâhdar at the same moment that the rebel leader sighted them and shouted fiercely to them to halt.

Home went the spurs yet once again, the tired horses snorted as they bounded off the heath on to the glaring road, and away went the three, with the *sowârs* in full pursuit. Chaloner whipped out his sword and, in his excitement, turned in his saddle and shook the weapon at his pursuers, shouting his defiance as he rode; but this was a dangerous form of entertainment which he soon gave up, and he turned his attention to the task of keeping his tired charger on its feet.

Fortunately for the fugitives, the Pandies either had not their carbines loaded or else forgot to use them; for although each expected momentarily to feel a bullet between his shoulders, the seconds passed with no other sound than the thunderous pounding of hoofs in the rear, coming, however, gradually closer and closer, as Chaloner could tell without looking round.

And now signs of movement and excitement could be seen around the Kashmir Gate. A red coat or two could be seen flitting hither and thither above the bastion—thank God the city was still in the hands of the British!—and presently the figure of an officer, running, appeared in the road, just outside the portcullis, evidently wondering what on earth was happening.

"Get ready to close the gates!" almost screamed

Chaloner as they approached. "The native troops have mutinied and those fellows behind are pursuing us!"

But the beat of the horses' hoofs drowned his words, and the red-coated lieutenant in charge of the gate still remained standing there, too astonished and puzzled to move.

Then at last the true state of affairs seemed to dawn on him—for one of the *sowârs* had drawn a pistol and fired at the three horsemen, hoping at the very last moment to prevent their escape, and he shouted some words to the little detachment of red-coats on the bastion, and commenced himself to run back through the gate. The last thing that Chaloner and his companion saw, as they flashed through the opening, was a puff of smoke from one of the soldier's muskets up above, and a twinkling of red as the members of the gate-guard came tumbling down the steps in response to their officer's command. There was a yell, a crash on the road behind, and the fugitives knew that one at least of their pursuers had met with his deserts.

Then they were inside the city, shouting to the young lieutenant the news of the rising at Mirapur, as they slid from the backs of their almost foundered horses, and begging him, as he valued his life and the lives of all in Delhi, to shut the massive Kashmir Gate. And, to add point to their request, they themselves rushed to assist the guard to close the valves.

But, unfortunately, they were just a few seconds too late.

Before the heavy doors could be properly set in motion the first of the mutineer *sowârs* were through, and at once commenced sabring the men who were trying to keep them out. One huge cavalryman rode straight at the Subâhdar, and Shere Singh would have ended his career there and then had it not been for Chaloner's pistol, which brought the fellow down even as the vicious blow was falling.

The moment that the British soldiers realized it was not possible to keep the enemy out, they seized their muskets, and, fixing bayonets, strove to keep the *sowârs* at bay; but they were hopelessly outnumbered, and it was soon evident that unless reinforcements arrived quickly the guard would be "wiped out" entirely, and the gate—and consequently Delhi itself—would fall into the hands of the mutineers.

The young lieutenant very soon realized this important fact, and shouted to Chaloner to draw off his two friends and ride as hard as they could to the Mori Bastion for help, while he, together with his fast-diminishing force, would do his best to prevent the mutineers from pursuing them, and would also endeavour to hold the gate until assistance could be sent.

Unwilling as Chaloner was to leave a comrade in so precarious a situation, he quite understood the wisdom of the lieutenant's advice. To take Fairbanks and Shere Singh with him was also advisable, for sounds of turmoil were already beginning to make themselves heard in that quarter of the city, and one man alone might be pulled down and torn to pieces before he could reach the bastion.

He therefore called both his friends by name, and, while the officer and the guard kept the *sowârs* at bay to the best of their ability, the three mounted again and rode at full speed for that help which was so urgently needed at the Kashmir Gate.

CHAPTER IV

"Death hovers over this City!"

No sooner had the three horsemen left the Kashmir Gate and entered the winding, narrow streets of the city which lay immediately inside the walls, and which it was necessary for them to traverse in order to reach the Mori Bastion, than they realized that, in that mysterious manner known only to Hindus and certain savage races, the news of the successful rising at Mirapur was already known in Delhi, and that the natives had already begun the practices which had been carried out in Mirapur itself, the British, strive as they might, being in altogether insufficient numbers to bring the offenders to book.

The British authorities in the city were of course aware that trouble of some sort was in the air, but they had had no inkling of the magnitude or serious nature of that trouble until Chaloner and his friends rode in with the news. Even then, with their fatal blind faith in the native army, the officials found it exceedingly difficult to believe that the disturbance was anything more serious than a temporary upheaval, due, perhaps, to over-indulgence, on the part of some of the sepoys, in *bhang* or some other intoxicating and exciting drug.

When, however, appeals for assistance and protection began to pour in to the various British detachments scattered about the city—appeals for protection against murder and outrage, pillage and burning—when the officers could see for themselves the glow of flames proceeding from the direction in which the British quarter lay, and when, at last, their own compatriots, in some cases their own kith and kin, actually claimed refuge in the soldiers' quarters—then, but not until then, did the authorities awake to the fact that here was no harmless, temporary excitement, but mutiny itself, in very deed, raising its grim and terrible head of menace over all India.

As has been mentioned above, however, the natives had, in some manner—possibly by means of the *chuppati* signal—become aware of the true state of affairs almost as soon as the train was lighted in Mirapur. They had been gradually becoming bolder and bolder, less and less careful ot consequences, ever since, until by the time that the three messengers arrived in Delhi the streets, in the less reputable parts of the city at least, were already seething with the bazar rabble; with criminals who, at other times, dared not show their faces by daylight; and even, here and there, with red-coated sepoys and grey-frocked *sowârs*, who had already thrown off their allegiance and joined hands with the *badmâshes* in the work of pillage and rapine.

Shere Singh, who seemed to know something of every city in that part of India, volunteered to lead the way to the bastion, and they proceeded in the same order in which they had ridden in from Mirapur; but the horses were tired out, the streets were already thronged with people, and their progress was both slow and dangerous. The natives were aware that a fight was taking place round the Kashmir Gate, aware, too, that these three were going for help; but, there being no native troops among this particular crowd, they could not summon up sufficient courage actually to attack the three grim-visaged horsemen who rode steadily through them, with their long, sharp swords bare in their right hands, although they hindered them in every way they possibly could, short of deliberate assault.

But, little by little, by a free use of the spur and a plentiful application of the flat of their swords across the shoulders of the more obstreperous, the messengers gradually forced their way onward, although they were all already bleeding from wounds caused by stones, broken bottles, and other flying missiles which came hurtling through the air from the outskirts of the crowd and from the upper windows of the hovels that lined the streets.

The fiery Shere Singh kept his temper admirably, for he knew that if he once lost it, and began to use the edge of his weapon, the crowd would demand blood for blood, would take their courage in both hands, and, acting in unison, tear them from their saddles and rend them limb from limb. It was only by dint of patience and unlimited forbearance that they could hope to win through; and the Subâhdar whispered that fact to his companions, warning them not to strike until such action became absolutely necessary in self-defence. If, he said, such a course became necessary, they must try to urge their horses abreast of his, so as to form a front to the enemy and protect one another's flanks. Riding in single file, as they were doing now, would simply mean that the mob would be able to tear them down and slay them one by one.

And indeed it began to appear as though that time were rapidly approaching; for, in addition to stones and other missiles, knives were now beginning to flash through the air, and several natives, of the more truculent sort, were already striving to force a way up to the horsemen, the daggers in their hands and the scowls of hatred on their faces being sufficient evidence of their intentions. Also, the crowd was closing in so thickly in front of them that almost their only chance of freeing themselves lay in cutting a way through with their swords: for it would be fatal to allow their horses to come to a standstill; that would certainly mean the signal for a concerted attack.

Shere Singh measured the situation carefully with a wary eye, and noticed that, here and there, red and grey coats were beginning to appear, attracted by the uproar.

To hesitate any longer would be folly—suicide—and quickly turning in his saddle he called to the others to form into line.

With an effort the two lads forced their horses, by hand, spur, and voice, over the space that separated them from the Subâhdar, and the next instant were alongside him, Chaloner on his right, Fairbanks on his left; and now the swords of all three began to flash in the morning sunlight, and their spurs to glisten red.

They must win through at all costs!

With a shriek of pain and despair a savage-looking man with a long knife went down before Shere Singh's *tulwâr*, and two more fell to the points of Chaloner and Fairbanks, while a shrill cry of rage arose from the crowd, mingled with cries of: "They are spies! They are *Farângis* disguised! Down with them! Kill the dogs! See, the young one on the right uses a *Farângi* officer's sword; he is no true *sowâr*. Pull him from his horse, brothers, and tear him limb from limb. Those others, too; one is the Subâhdar Shere Singh, the dog who fights against his own comrades, and the other is a *Farângi*, for all his dark skin." This last from a grey-coated *sowâr* who was desperately pushing a way through the crowd, a naked sword in his hand. "*Ai!* let *me* come at him, brothers, and I will——"

But what he would have done remained a mystery; for Chaloner, recognizing that the *sowâr* was becoming a rallying-point, a leader, drew his pistol, luckily loaded, from his belt, and shot the fellow through the head before he could get near enough to use his sword. Fairbanks did the same to another *badmâsh*, who had seized his bridle and was trying to pull his horse to its knees.

A cry of rage again shrilled forth, but the crowd was learning that the three horsemen were desperate, and that it meant death to come within the swing of their swords.

Those in front of the horses gave back a little, leaving a clear space of a few yards, and in an instant the riders utilized the opportunity to urge their nags forward.

Driving in their spurs they struck the front ranks of the crowd like a thunder-bolt and crashed through into its middle by the sheer weight of their impetus, the horses themselves, excited by the smell of blood and the cries of the natives, entering into the struggle with as much energy as their masters, trampling down men with their iron-shod hoofs, even seizing them with their teeth and shaking the miserable wretches as a dog shakes a rat.

This was an experience new to the bazar-dwelling rabble, and the cry arose: "*Wah illah*! brothers, let them go; they are bewitched, bewitched! Even their horses fight for them; they are the children of *Sheitân*! *Ai! Ai!*"

"Children of *Sheitân* are we indeed, as ye shall learn, ye bazar-born dogs!" thundered Shere Singh in a voice that dominated the rest of the cries like the note of a bugle; "disperse, ye cattle thieves, eaters of swines' flesh, disperse!" And his great sword, with those of his companions, rose and fell with the regularity of a machine, dealing out death unsparingly.

The crowd hesitated a fraction of a second, and then broke, its members fleeing in all directions to escape the deadly blades which seemed to follow them everywhere.

The three had won through, in spite of all obstacles, and the road was clear so far as the Mori Bastion, which they now saw rising in front of them at a bend in the street.

But where, Chaloner asked himself, were the redcoats who should have been on guard at the gate? The crowd through which he had just cut his way had been making outcry enough, one would have thought, to alarm the whole city; yet there was not a sign of a soldier anywhere about. Shere Singh, too, appeared to share his apprehensions, for he was staring anxiously before him, as though searching for signs that the bastion was still in the possession of the British.

"Chaloner Sahib," he exclaimed, "I see no traces of your countrymen here; I am afraid we shall obtain no help at the Mori Bastion. They have either all been killed or have departed to defend some other part of the town."

"Heaven help those poor fellows at the Kashmir Gate, if that is the case!" replied Chaloner. "Succour will never reach them if we cannot get assistance here. Even now, I fear, it would be too late: we have been so long on our way. I expect the gate is already in the hands of the enemy!"

Their suspicions proved, alas! only too well founded.

On their arrival at the bastion Chaloner slipped off his horse and ran up the winding stair, while the others remained below on guard; but there was no living soul on the premises. Several dreadfully mutilated corpses of British soldiers lay in the chamber above the gate and on the stairs, and Chaloner was forced to the conclusion that there had been a fight here, and that the officer of the guard, finding the place could not be defended against such overwhelming numbers, had cut his way out and retreated to some other bastion or gate, where he would possibly find a stronger force of British soldiery.

This surmise of Chaloner's was as a matter of fact correct. The officer had been attacked about the time that the fight began round the Kashmir Gate, and after losing several men had come to the conclusion that the only thing left for him was to withdraw. This he had done, and had managed to reach the Kabul Gate, a quarter of a mile away, with a small remnant of his force, where he joined hands with the lieutenant in charge there, and awaited events amid a chaos in which his whole world appeared to be tumbling about his ears.

But Chaloner did not know this, could not, of course, guess in which direction the little force had gone, and was now reluctantly compelled to come to the conclusion that he could do nothing to assist the guard at the Kashmir Gate or help to save it from capture. It was manifestly impossible for the three to make their way back there again; and, even if they could, a reinforcement so small would be absolutely useless; it would merely be throwing their lives away. The question therefore remained, what was to be done next?

"It is no use stopping here, that's clear," observed Chaloner, as soon as he had completed his exploration; "there is nobody here to send to the assistance of those poor beggars at the other gate, and it's no use thinking of trying to get back ourselves. If we remain here we shall be spotted by that crowd we had to fight our way through just now, and if they see that we are unsupported they'll be after us like a shot. Subâhdar Sahib, you know Delhi better than I do; where do you think we shall be most likely to find some of our own troops?"

The Subâhdar shook his head. "It is difficult to say, with things as they are now, *Huzoor*," he replied. "They may still be scattered about at the various guard-houses, or they may by this time have taken the alarm and massed their forces in some one place; which would be much the safest plan. But where they would be most likely to collect I cannot say; perhaps at the fort, perhaps at the magazine, perhaps at the Residency, or the Court-house—I don't know. It might be best for us——"

"Whatever you two intend doing," interupted Fairbanks, "I am quite clear in my own mind where *I* am going, and that is to the telegraph office, if I can find it. You remember that last night I tried to telegraph to here from Mirapur, but found the line cut. Well, unless I can send the news of the rising away from here before the instruments are broken, or the line cut, it may be days before the true facts of the case are known to the rest of India, and heaven only knows what headway this mutiny may gain unless it is checked soon."

"That's a good idea indeed, Fairbanks," replied Chaloner, "always supposing that the operator here has not already done so. But I believe the office is some distance outside the walls, and if we once get out, we may find it impossible to get back again."

"Your pardon, *Huzoor*," broke in Shere Singh. "Although there is, as you say, an office outside, there is also one not far from here, and I can lead you to it."

"Bravo, Subâhdar Sahib!" exclaimed Fairbanks, "I thought as much. As for your suggestion, Peter, that the proper operator may already have sent—well—he may, of course; but you know it was only just after our own arrival that our people began to wake up to the fact that there was anything very wrong, and I think it exceedingly likely that the rebels here may have taken the precaution to kill him before he could send any message—or, as they did at Mirapur, may have cut the line. If they have done that, I must reach the other office at all costs, and try to get through from there."

"Very well, then," said Chaloner. "If that's your idea, we shall, of course, accompany you; we must all keep together, that's certain, for we could never be sure of finding one another again in this rabbit-warren of a place. So lead on, Shere Singh, as fast as you please."

"Stay a moment, sahibs," replied the Subâhdar, dismounting. "If ye will be advised by me, ye will abandon the horses, and go henceforth on foot. Our horses are known here now, and soon hundreds will be looking for three mounted men resembling ourselves. On foot we stand less chance of being recognized; and also, we shall have to go into hiding if we are to remain here long, and we could not do that if we were encumbered by the animals."

"That is a true word, Subâhdar Sahib," agreed Chaloner; "but I hate the idea of abandoning poor old Don. Is there nowhere we could hide the beasts?"

"Doubtless we could, *Huzoor*," replied Shere Singh; "but who is to say when we might have opportunity to feed and water them? Suppose we fastened them up, and circumstances prevented us leaving our hiding-place for two or three days, what would happen to them then?"

Chaloner shuddered at the picture conjured up by the Sikh. "I had not thought of that, Shere Singh," he said. "There is, of course, only the one course left for us to pursue; but, first of all, let us remove all their trappings, and so give them the best chance we can."

So said, so done, and five minutes later, after all three had said a last word of farewell to the faithful creatures which had served them so long and so well, and after hiding saddles and bridles behind a clump of bushes near the bastion, they plunged again, under the leadership of the Subâhdar, into a side alley, where they hoped to be screened from observation, and by way of which, Shere Singh said, they could arrive at the telegraph office.

Keeping close to the walls, and darting swiftly across the cross streets which they had to pass, they made their way unobserved into the street in which the office was situated; which street, fortunately, lay some distance away from that where their encounter with the mob had taken place, so that, with any luck at all, they hoped that nobody would recognize them for what they were.

Here they found the place swarming with rebel soldiers, both horse and foot, for the most part hopelessly intoxicated; for looting of the liquor shops had now been in progress for some time, this being the first thing to which the mutineers had turned their attention. And this fact was no doubt of great assistance to the trio, since the mutineers were too fuddled to pay much heed to anything but the business of guiding their own footsteps.

True, they were several times accosted by parties of drunken soldiery, who invited them to share their orgies; but a few jesting words from either Shere Singh or from Fairbanks, who spoke the language like a native, were sufficient to send the mutineers on their way laughing, without their suspicions being in the least degree aroused.

Presently they arrived opposite the office, which stood

at a corner of two streets, and a hasty glance as they strolled past was sufficient to show them that there were no sepoys within; but at that particular moment the street was so crowded at that point that attention would certainly have been attracted had they entered just then, and the success of their scheme depended upon their being left absolutely alone to the work they desired to carry out. Therefore they strolled slowly onward, now and then looking behind them to see whether matters had improved.

"I saw nobody inside," remarked Fairbanks in a low tone; "but of course that was only to be expected. The operator would be certain to seek refuge somewhere as soon as his duty was done. I only hope that he *was* able to do it before he left, or—before they discovered him."

"Now, sahibs, *now*!" exclaimed Shere Singh, as they were repassing the office for the fourth time. "If we are quick we can manage it now."

And, suiting the action to the word, he darted inside, followed instantly by the two lads.

Once inside, Chaloner shut the door silently and shot the bolts, trusting that nobody would notice what had been done, but determined that, if they did, they should be delayed from entering as long as possible. Fairbanks lost not a moment, but dashed straight to the counter, raised the flap, and sprang toward the instrument on a table behind.

A sharp exclamation, a stumble, and then a heavy fall made Chaloner's and Shere Singh's hearts leap into their throats, and their hands to their hilts. But before they could reach Fairbanks, to help him to rise, they heard his voice exclaiming softly:

"All right, Peter, all right! I'm not hurt. But what I feared has certainly happened. I have just fallen over the body of the operator, and from the feel of him

I should say that he has been dead several hours. I am afraid he could never have sent that message, poor fellow, for, apparently, he has been cut down from behind while sitting at the table. He would have had no reason to expect the blow, and probably he never knew what killed him. We'll soon see, however," he went on, placing his fingers on the keys and commencing to tap, tap, tap the call for the operator at the other end of the line, wherever that might be.

Chaloner has since acknowledged that the ensuing few minutes—while they were waiting for a reply, not knowing at what moment there might come a thunderous summons at the door; not knowing whether Fairbanks's call would be responded to—were among the longest he has ever experienced. The time seemed to drag itself out into a veritable eternity, and at length he actually began to comfort himself with the thought that surely darkness would soon be upon them, and that their movements would be shielded by the friendly night. As a matter of fact, Shere Singh, who was not nearly so highly strung, afterwards declared that the period of waiting was not a minute longer than a quarter of an hour.

"Tap, tap, tap", went Fairbanks's key again, impatiently this time, for he was beginning to fear that the line must be cut somewhere. The instrument itself was certainly undamaged, as his experienced eye could tell at a glance.

"Either the line has been cut," the clerk whispered presently, "or the operator has not yet come down to his office. If the latter is the case, they certainly know nothing about this rising at the other end. If they had the slightest suspicion, the operator would be standing by his instrument now, either sending or waiting for news. Ah!" he broke off suddenly, as the needle in front of him suddenly ceased to click, "there is somebody there at last, thank goodness! Peter, if you have a bit of paper and a pencil, please take down the conversation as I call it out; it may be extremely valuable in the future. Got it? All right, then; listen! I'm just receiving this communication.

"'Hillo! who's the funny man at your end of the line? I suppose you think it no end of a joke to get down to the office and begin to worry the life out of a fellow at this early hour—in the hot weather too.'

"Now my reply, Peter.

"'Hillo! Listen carefully. I am not joking with you; I'm in deadly earnest. But, first of all, what station am I talking to?'

"'Why, Lahore, of course. You ought to know that. But by your excited manner of operating you appear to have news of importance to tell. What is it?'"

Fairbanks had just turned to Chaloner to ask him whether he had "got that down", when Shere Singh, who had been peeping through the close wire mesh which protected the interior of the office from the public gaze, suddenly darted back, on tiptoe, to the side of the two lads. "*Huzoors*," he whispered excitedly, "for the sake of Allah, hasten! Some of those *badmâshes* in the street have noticed that the door is closed, and there is quite a crowd collected outside now. In a few seconds they will try the door and, when they find it locked, will break it down. Our escape by the front is cut off now, but if we go at once we may be able to find some way out at the back, or over the flat roofs."

"Phew!" whistled Fairbanks. "That's bad. But we *must* send the news before we leave." And his fingers again commenced tapping frenziedly at the key.

"The native troops," he telegraphed, "have mutinied at Mirapur, slaughtering many Europeans, and have now come on to Delhi. Mutiny has broken out here also, and the rebels are at this moment murdering the English. Many of the bungalows in the European quarter have already been burned, and——"

At this moment the handle of the office door was turned, and almost simultaneously the building itself shook with the thunder of rifle butts beating upon the thin panels of the door. The mob had evidently become suspicious, and were going to investigate matters, and if the three were to save themselves there was not a moment to lose, for the door was already beginning to splinter under the savage blows.

Without a second's hesitation the Subâhdar unceremoniously grabbed Fairbanks by the arm and pulled him away from the instrument, hustling him and Chaloner through a little door behind the counter, leading he knew not where; and as he closed and locked it behind them, Fairbanks caught the sound of the needle of the telegraph instrument clicking, as the man at Lahore begged frantically: "Repeat! repeat!"

In the histories of the Indian Mutiny the tale has often been told how the operator at Delhi stuck to his instrument, and sent the warning far and wide, until he was found and slain by the mutineers; but, as an actual fact, it was Fairbanks, the Mirapur clerk, who sent the message, which was afterwards telegraphed from Lahore all over the country, giving warning of what was occurring, and who consequently saved India. The Delhi clerk, poor fellow, to whom the brave act was credited, was never given the chance to send the warning, for he had died in ignorance of the terrible truth; or perhaps he may have obtained an inkling of it, and have been on the point of dispatching the news when he was cut down. At any rate he did not send it, since the Lahore operator was unaware of anything wrong until he heard from Fairbanks, who naturally saved time by using the line that was already connected with the Delhi instrument, which was, as we have seen, that to Lahore.

As soon as the Subâhdar had locked the door behind him, the three found themselves in a narrow, dark, stone-flagged passage, evidently connecting, on the left hand, with the outer door opening into the side street, which they had noticed at their first examination of the building; but it would be too dangerous to try to escape by that way, since the office was at the corner, and the crowd besieging the front door would be certain to discover them.

They turned to the right, therefore, and ran stumbling along in the gloom for a few yards, until Chaloner, who was leading, tripped at the bottom of a flight of stone steps. He was up again in a moment, however, and led the way upward, the light becoming stronger every second, until, before they were aware of the fact, they had emerged upon the flat roofs of the row of buildings of which the telegraph office was one.

As they did so they heard the crash beneath them which announced that at last the front door had given way, and that the mob was hard upon their heels.

Fortunately for the fugitives, the front part of this particular row of houses was provided with a kind of ornamental parapet of solid stonework, and this served to protect them from observation by the people in the street below; so that, by keeping well to the back part of the roofs, they were able to walk upright, instead of having to crawl, as would otherwise have been the case.

They took the fullest advantage of this piece of good fortune by running at the top of their speed, so as to put as much ground between themselves and their pursuers as possible; but they knew that it would only be a question of seconds before the mob, guessing which way they had gone, would appear on the roofs behind them. Before that could happen they must find some place of concealment or some method of descending from the roofs to the alley which ran along the back of the buildings, and which, luckily, happened to be quite deserted.

Their star was decidedly in the ascendant that morning. While they were expecting, every second, to hear the wild shout behind them which should tell that they had been sighted, Chaloner saw, close before him, an iron handrail, showing that there was a flight of steps leading down from that particular roof.

He made for the spot at top speed, and plunged down the stairs, four or five steps at a time, closely followed by Shere Singh and Fairbanks; and in a few seconds they found themselves safely out of sight in the narrow lane below.

"Which way now?" gasped Chaloner, panting for breath and streaming with perspiration.

The Subâhdar paused an instant as though to verify his bearings. Then: "This way, sahibs. I think I know a place where we can hide until dark." And away they went again, down another lane at right angles to the one in which they were standing.

Luck favoured them here too. They met not a soul, probably because the majority of the inhabitants were engaged in slaying and looting in the richer parts of the city, and after a hard five minutes' run they stopped opposite a backdoor leading into a garden, at the other end of which was a white stone house of considerable size.

"The house of the Collector Sahib, *Huzoors*," whispered Shere Singh. "It is a large one, and if none of the *badmâshes* are there already we shall find it a very good hiding-place."

"The Collector!" exclaimed Chaloner eagerly. "They

will hardly have dared to attack *him*. We shall surely find refuge here."

"Deceive not thyself, *Huzoor*," replied Shere Singh solemnly. "If the Collector Sahib is indeed still here, I fear it is only his dead body that we shall find. He was not loved by the populace. He was a very hard man."

Without further words the Subâhdar pushed open the gate and entered the garden, aglow with flowers of many hues, and fruit; and threading their way among the trees, the three cautiously approached the silent building.

The lattice-work door at the back of the house stood open, and they entered unchallenged; but once inside they realized that Shere Singh had been a true prophet.

It would serve no good purpose to describe in detail the shocking sights that affronted their gaze in almost every room into which they penetrated; it is sufficient to say that, when they finally descended to the cellar, there to hide until darkness fell, they were all faint and sick with horror. Chaloner voiced the general opinion when he observed, in a hollow, lifeless tone: "Surely, surely the shadow of death hovers over this city!"

CHAPTER V

In the Collector's House

"*Allah! Allah!*" muttered the Subâhdar, for the tenth time. "Will this day *never* come to an end? It seems to me, Chaloner Sahib," he went on, addressing the young man, "as though we had been here a week, and, for my part, I am nearly mad with thirst."

Indeed, the temperature in that cellar was something terrible, recalling to both Englishmen the stories they had read in their youth about "The Black Hole of Calcutta". They could appreciate now the feelings of those unhappy beings who had been the victims of the bloodthirsty, inhuman Suraj-ud-Dowlah in 1756, just one hundred years previously. For eight long hours—which had seemed more like eighty—they had been crouching in that dark, sunless cellar, feeling like animals in a trap; for there was but one door to the place—that by which they had entered—and should the mob or a band of marauders take it into their heads to search the house, there was no way of escape, no backdoor like that at the telegraph office, through which they could slip away unobserved. Should their hiding-place be searched, all that would remain for them would be to place their backs to the wall and fight there, in the dark, until they were killed, or could effect their escape; for they were, one and all, resolved never to fall alive into the hands of the mutineers. The dreadful sights in the rooms above their heads had been sufficient to make them swear that no such ghastly fate should overtake them if they could possibly help it.

Time after time they had experienced all the horror and anxiety of a false alarm, hearing a shouting, howling mob halt either at the front or the back of the premises, and expecting every second that the *badmâshes* would decide to search the place afresh, or to use it, perchance, for an all-night orgy. But each time the danger had passed, leaving them pale of cheek and breathless with strain and apprehension, until, about three o'clock in the afternoon, the Subâhdar gave vent to the remark above recorded, which was heartily echoed by his two companions in misfortune. It did, indeed, seem as though the hours of daylight would never come to an end; and the lighting of a match, for about the twentieth time, told them, by referring to Chaloner's watch, that at least four hours more must elapse before it would be safe for them to venture forth.

"Cheer up, Subâhdar Sahib!" exclaimed Chaloner, as gaily as his parched tongue would permit. "Only four hours more to wait, and then you'll be able to drink to your heart's content. I too have been suffering severely for some time, and if it were not for—for what we saw above, when we came in, I should feel almost inclined to risk being seen, and go up there to see whether I could find some water. The heat of this place is simply intolerable!"

"I would not do that, *Huzoor*, if I were you," replied Shere Singh; "but—perhaps one of us might risk going into the garden, and bringing in some fruit. That would be both food and drink, and would keep us going until we could get something more satisfying."

"That's a good idea," agreed Chaloner. "I'll try it myself now. If I take a careful look round before leaving the shadow of the door I ought to be able to make the excursion without being seen. Now that you've mentioned fruit, Shere Singh, I really don't think I can wait any longer." And he rose stiffly to his feet.

Shere Singh laid a hand on his arm.

"Nay, heaven-born," he said in a low tone, "it is not for thee to do this thing, but for thy servant. I look more like a native than do either of ye, *Huzoors*, in spite of your stained skins, and if I am seen or spoken to I can perhaps disarm suspicion better than ye. They would know thee for a *Farângi* at once, Chaloner Sahib, by thy Ûrdu," he smiled, "which—forgive me—thou speakest not over-well."

"Well, how about me, then, Subâhdar Sahib?" croaked another voice from a corner—Fairbanks's. "I speak Ûrdu as well as thou, thou old boaster. Why should not I go?"

"Nay, nay, sahib," replied Shere Singh. "For many reasons the duty lies with me. Seek not to hinder me, for my mind is made up."

"So be it," answered Chaloner. "*Hûkm hai!*" (It is an order!) But be not long, or we shall come to look for thee. Thou art far too valuable a man to lose lightly."

The Subâhdar smiled, well pleased at the praise from his beloved sahib. "I will be quick as the messenger of Takandûr (Alexander the Great), *Huzoor*," he said. "Be not fearful for me; my hour is not yet come." And with these words he silently faded from the cellar, the slight sound of the door at the stair-head opening and the accompanying momentary gleam of light being the only evidences of his departure. The door closed noiselessly behind him, and the two lads were left in the darkness, anxiously to await his return.

Scarcely a minute seemed to have elapsed before they heard a sound in the room above, as of a man walking rapidly across the floor, followed immediately by a stumble, a fall, and the muffled echo of an Ûrdu execration.

"Confound Shere Singh!" exclaimed Chaloner angrily, his temper somewhat on edge from the discomfort he was enduring. "The clumsy beggar will rouse the whole neighbourhood if he's not careful. He hasn't been long though. I'll say that for him."

To his astonishment he heard, from the corner where Fairbanks was lying, the sound of an excited "Hush!"

"'Hush!' Why 'hush'?" he repeated, lowering his voice however. "It's only Shere Singh coming back, and our voices could hardly be heard in the street, even if we shouted."

"For Heaven's sake be quiet!" again urged Fairbanks. "You silly idiot! *Can't you hear that that is not Shere Singh?*"

Chaloner's heart leaped into his throat. What a fool he was, to be sure! Of course the Subâhdar would have been particularly careful to make no sound; and, besides, now he came to think of it, those quick, heavy footfalls were quite unlike Shere Singh's customary cat-like tread. But if the man above were not the Subâhdar, who, in the name of everything that was unlucky, could he be? Certainly no one else but one of the *badmâshes*; or, perchance, a mutineer who had left his companions, and had sneaked back to obtain some extra loot, or some article that had taken his fancy at his first visit.

The predicament of the two Englishmen in the cellar was a terrible one. They dared not move from their hiding-place, since they could not be sure whether the man in the room above were by himself or had some of his fellow-scoundrels with him; there was no earthly means whereby they could warn Shere Singh, who all this time was probably gathering fruit in the garden, quite unconscions of the peril hovering over him; and if he were not warned, he would most likely walk right into the arms of the man, or men, and be slain before he could recover from his surprise. Up above, too, after the first sound, nothing further had been heard; and Chaloner pictured the "Pandy" as having caught sight of Shere Singh, and as waiting behind a door, or a curtain, to stab him as he went past. The perspiration poured from his forehead, and he clenched his hands in an agony of apprehension, What, oh! what could be done to save the Subâhdar?

And then, with startling suddenness, the period of suspense came to an end.

There was an exclamation of surprise, this time undoubtedly in the Subâhdar's well-known tones, immediately followed by a shout of anger and alarm in the accents of the person who had previously exclaimed in the room above.

There followed a hurried trampling of feet, and the crash of overturning furniture; and then footsteps were heard flying from one part of the room to the other, heavy, clumsy footfalls, always with the light, cat-like tread of Shere Singh following them wherever they went; and both Fairbanks and Chaloner breathed more freely on hearing these sounds, for from them they were able to picture in their minds exactly what was taking place above, and knew that, unless people from the street were attracted by the disturbance, the Subâhdar stood in very little danger.

Evidently he had come silently back into the room with his armful of fruit—for they had heard it drop on the floor—had caught sight of the intruder, probably helping himself to some of the property of the late owner of the house, and had at once dashed at the man to prevent his escape. The fellow had seen or heard him coming, had sprung back, upsetting a chair or some other article of furniture, and a chase round the spacious room was now in progress, the mutineer striving to gain one of the doors and escape, and the Subâhdar straining every nerve to prevent him; since, if the fellow got away, it would be tantamount to the signature of a death warrant for all three of them.

"Look here, Fairbanks," exclaimed Chaloner to his friend, "I have no doubt Shere Singh can deal with that fellow single-handed, since there appears to be only one of him, but nevertheless I'm going to take a hand in the affair myself, and try to bring it to a close as soon as possible; for if this row goes on much longer, attention is sure to be attracted. Listen! He finds there is no escape, and is beginning to call for help. Quick, or we shall have the mob about our ears again in no time."

Without a word, Fairbanks sprang to his feet, unsheathed his sword, as Chaloner had already done, and followed his friend headlong up the cellar stairs. And then came a check.

They had forgotten that Shere Singh had locked the door behind him!

"Both together!" exclaimed the elder lad in a low tone, knowing that his chum would understand; and their shoulders crashed simultaneously against the frail door, which at once gave way, allowing them to sprawl headlong into the passage leading to the back room. At the same time they heard Shere Singh's voice exclaiming: "Is that you, sahibs?"

"We come, Subâhdar Sahib," was the reply, and they dashed together, sword in hand, into the chamber.

Here they saw the native officer, swinging his *tulwâr* menacingly, eyeing a red-coated mutineer sepoy, armed with a musket, with a bayonet at the end, the weapon being evidently unloaded, since he had not shot at the Subâhdar.

The Pandy was visibly in the last stage of terror, and had entrenched himself behind a large piano, over the top of which the wicked-looking bayonet protruded. They had evidently been circling round the room, and round the instrument, until the sepoy was out of breath; and now, as a last hope, he had started shouting, at the top of as much voice as remained to him, for help. Shere Singh was debating, apparently, on the best method of reaching him, and putting an end to his cries, when the Englishmen darted into the room.

The sepoy, however, noticing their dark faces and their *sowâr* uniform, imagined that they were mutineer cavalry-men who had come in answer to his calls for help, and, pointing to the tall Subâhdar, gasped out: "Ha! brothers; ye have come just in time. Slay me that dog yonder. He is a friend of the *Farângis*. I know him well. They say he rode in from Mirapur this very morning, with two disguised *Farângis*, whom our noble friends very nearly caught and slew. They escaped, but we shall have them soon. Do not hesitate, brothers; ye are two to one, and——"

Then, seeing the eyes of the two supposed *sowârs* fixed sternly upon him, and observing that Shere Singh made no motion to defend himself, the truth began to dawn upon the trapped wretch, and his speech ended suddenly, his lower lip drooped, and the musket slipped from his trembling grasp and clattered noisily to the floor.

Without a word Shere Singh stepped forward and raised his sword, while the sepoy fell upon his knees crying: "*Marf karo! Marf karo!*" (Have mercy! have mercy!)

Fairbanks and Chaloner would have preferred to spare the man's life, could his silence have been ensured; but of this there was no possibility. His promise could not be relied upon for an instant, and to bind and gag him and hide him away in some part of the house would have been tantamount to condemning him to death by slow starvation, since they could not reckon on being able to return to the place once they had left it that evening. No, unfortunately, mercy was an utter impossibilty in this case, and the man must resign himself to meet a fate which he would gladly have meted out to the other three had they been in his power.

The Subâhdar, too, had his own opinion on the matter, and did not intend to consult his British comrades in this case. He knew the only thing to be done, and intended to do it. His life and the lives of his friends were worth a great deal more than that of the bloodthirsty, cringing wretch before him, whose hands were already dyed with the blood of the family whose home that house had been.

At the last moment the two lads turned their heads away; they could kill with the best, in the heat of strife, but a cold-blooded execution, however richly deserved, they could not witness.

There was the sound of a dull, heavy blow, a curious hissing noise, and some heavy object rolled to a far corner of the room, while the body itself collapsed upon the soft Persian carpet with a thud.

When they again glanced round, rather white and shaken, they found that Shere Singh had flung a large, coloured tablecloth over the trunk, and that he was wrapping the smaller object round in a curtain which he had pulled from its pole.

"Now, *Huzoors*," exclaimed Shere Singh, "we have no time to lose. We must carry this," touching the corpse with his foot, "away and hide it somewhere; for it is possible that his cries may have attracted attention, and that we shall have his friends coming to look for him before long. If you two sahibs will take one end of this cloth I will carry the other and the—the bundle, and we will remove the body upstairs and lock it into a cupboard if we can find one."

The two lads realized the necessity for immediate action, and obeyed without a word. A cupboard such as they needed was found at the very top of the building, right under the roof, and here they left their gruesome burden, locking the door afterwards and throwing the key into the garden. Then they returned to the room where the struggle had taken place, re-arranged the furniture as it had been when they entered, and put things straight again. The pool of blood which had flowed from the sepoy's body they were obliged to leave, trusting that it would soon dry in the hot atmosphere, after which it would not be particularly noticeable among the other horrors with which the room was filled.

This done, they repaired, as best they could, the broken lock on the cellar door, and then gathered up the fruit which Shere Singh had plucked, and retired below to satisfy the hunger and thirst with which they were all consumed.

"Let us thank Heaven," observed Chaloner, as soon as they were in a fit condition for conversation, "that that danger has passed us at any rate. When I heard that fellow above, and realized that it was not you, Subâhdar Sahib, I feared for a moment that it was all up with us. We have been fortunate indeed."

Shere Singh saw, as yet, not so much reason for rejoicing.

"*Ai, Ai, Huzoor!*" he observed slowly. "That is all very well; but we are not yet out of the wood—far from it. In fact, we are in more danger than ever now. That fellow's friends will miss him before long, if they haven't done so already. They will be sure to guess that he has come back here to get more pillage, since he probably sneaked off alone, and they will be along to look for him shortly, that is certain. I would to Allah that it were dark, so that we could leave this house of death. I have a feeling in my heart that I shall meet my fate in this city, and that my time is not far distant, and I only pray that I may see you safe, sahibs, before I die."

"Say not so, Subâhdar Sahib," exclaimed both young men together. "Thou art, perchance, tired and overwrought, as are we. Let not thy mind dwell upon such fancies, man. Why, to-morrow, when we are safely among our friends, the British troops, thou wilt laugh at thy dismal forebodings!"

"Maybe, *Huzoors*, maybe," replied the old man, with a sigh; "but I think not. Also, be not yet too sure that there will be any British troops left for you and me to take refuge with. The garrison was small before; I trow it is smaller still now, and by to-morrow—who knows?—it may be gone altogether."

"We will hope not, Subâhdar Sahib," broke in Fairbanks. "By God's goodness I was enabled to telegraph the news, and you may be sure it is known all over India by now. In a few days every British soldier will be on the march, and this mutiny will die before it is yet full-born."

Shere Singh shook his head in the darkness. He knew, far better than his young friends, the extent to which the mutiny was likely to have spread already, and that it would need much British blood and treasure to be spent before the flame could be stamped out. But he was not going to damp their young ardour; they would need all they possessed, and more, in the days that were to come. He kept silent, and allowed Fairbanks's observation to pass unchallenged.

He sat for some time wrapped in thought while the two Englishmen were still satisfying healthy young appetites with the remainder of the fruit, and was at last about to ask Chaloner to strike a match and look at the time, when his quick ear, trained through long practice to note the smallest sound, caught a slight noise, somewhere in, or close to, the house, and his whole being was on the alert in an instant. Chaloner and Fairbanks were quite startled when he touched them both softly on the arm and bade them keep silent for their lives, as there was danger in the air.

They listened attentively, but could not detect the slightest sound, and were on the point of whispering to Shere Singh that he must have been mistaken, when, resounding like a cannon-shot to their alarmed ears, they heard the crash of the massive front-door slamming to, immediately followed by the tramp of numerous footsteps, and a perfect babel of voices in the room above their heads. The Subâhdar's apprehensions had proved true; what he feared had come to pass It was the sepoys who had arrived to look for their comrade, and who were shouting and trampling about up there; and—would that comrade's blood be dry by now, or would it still be fresh enough to attract their attention?

If it were, then they would inevitably search the house from top to bottom, and the three fugitives would be caught like rats in a trap.

With straining ears they listened for the shout, followed by the pause for examination, which should tell them that their secret had been discovered; and, sure enough, a few minutes later it came. There was a loud cry, a fierce chattering, and then a pause, full of menace. Instinctively the three fugitives crept closer together, laid their hands on their sword-hilts, and waited for the blows on the cellar door which should tell them that the end had arrived at last, and that Shere Singh's forebodings had come true.

Then there arose a perfect chorus of execration in Ûrdu, Tamil, and every dialect of India, followed by a rush of savage men across the room. They were coming, Chaloner told himself, and whipped his sword from its scabbard.

But no! There was to be a few minutes' respite at all events. The men had evidently decided that the slayer of their comrade, if still in the house, must be hiding in the upper stories, and thither they had gone. They would soon discover their error, however, and would be down again in no time; and then, surely, nothing could save the trio.

As the sounds decreased above, however, Shere Singh exclaimed hurriedly, out of the darkness: "Hast a match, Chaloner Sahib? If so, light it at once, so that we may see. Perhaps all is not lost even yet."

Chaloner hastily struck a light, and the primitive sulphur stick in use at that time gradually flared up, revealing, for the first time, the whole extent of the cellar.

It was bigger than they had anticipated, extending under the whole ground floor of the house, and they immediately started to explore, in the hope of finding some spot where they could secrete themselves. There were a number of big hogsheads, any of which would have been large enough to conceal a single man had they been empty; but they were all full, or nearly so, of stores of all descriptions; and, besides, if the sepoys came down they would be sure to look inside. No, they must seek some better place than that.

At last they found, just under the cellar door, and partly concealed behind the steps, a narrow opening, between the joists of the floor above and the surface of the solid earth out of which the cellar had been excavated, and into this it was just possible for the three of them to squeeze, if they lay flat upon their stomachs and dragged themselves as far inward as they could.

This they proceeded to do, covering themselves with dirt and cobwebs in the process, and full of apprehension lest they should disturb some sleeping cobra or other deadly reptile; and at last they lay fairly well concealed, their heads against a wall of earth and their feet almost at the outer edge of the ledge upon which they were extended.

They were reasonably safe, provided the sepoys did not search the cellar too thoroughly, or provided that their lights were not too brilliant; but there was no doubt that, if one of the mutineers happened to bring a torch anywhere near to where they lay, they could scarcely hope to avoid discovery. Chaloner also prayed that the smell of the sulphur matches he had lighted during the course of the day might not prove noticeable enough to arouse suspicion. Anyhow, he told himself, there they were, and there they must remain, now, until the end.

Happily for their nerves, their ordeal of waiting was not destined to be a very lengthy one. They had scarcely succeeded in squirming into their precarious place of concealment, making themselves as comfortable as circumstances would permit, when they plainly heard the sound of the sepoys descending the stairs. They were all chattering furiously, and their voices carried a savage, vindictive ring in their tones which informed the fugitives quite plainly that the headless body of the mutineer had been discovered by his comrades, and that the latter were determined to have revenge.

They were heard running through the rooms once more on the ground floor, wrecking furniture, pulling down hangings, and even ripping up the panelling of the walls with their bayonets, in their eagerness to discover the whereabouts of the hated enemy; and so long were they about the process that Chaloner was beginning to hope that the cellar door had escaped their scrutiny altogether.

And so it had up to then, and probably would have

done so altogether had not one of the marauders taken it into his head to pull down the curtain in the passage that concealed it, thinking that perhaps someone might be secreted in its folds.

As soon as the sepoy's eyes fell upon the door he twisted the handle savagely; but Shere Singh had effected his repair of the lock pretty thoroughly, and it did not give way.

The man therefore halloed to his companions, and in a few seconds the cellar was resounding with the strokes of musket butts upon the panels of the door. The mutineers were convinced that they had at last found the hiding-place of their quarry.

"Break it down, brothers!" shouted a voice, thick and hoarse with rum; "break it down. The accursed *Farângis* and that son of *Sheitân*"—Shere Singh gritted his teeth silently—"are somewhere down there, I'll swear. Say, comrades, what shall we do to the *sûrs* when we dig them out of their holes? Shall we treat them as we did the Collector Sahib's family, or shall we try something new?"

A roar of raucous laughter answered the inquirer, and a savage voice was making some unspeakable suggestion when the door gave way with a crash, and the foremost sepoys fell down the stone stairs with a rush, their friends on the top of them. There was a chorus of execration, the sound of a blow, and in a moment the mutineers had started a fight among themselves.

Had it not been so serious a predicament that they were all three in, Chaloner could have laughed at the episode; and as it was he was glad of the interlude, since it would serve to divert the minds of the ruffians from that smell of burnt matches which he was afraid they might notice.

Someone in authority here interposed and thrust the combatants apart, bidding them remember that they were not there to slay one another, but to slaughter the *Farângis*. The man who had been underneath, and whose arm appeared to have been broken, was ordered to take himself upstairs, the half-extinguished torch with which the leader had provided himself was picked up and fanned into a blaze again, and the search proceeded.

As Chaloner had foreseen, the open-topped hogsheads which had been used to keep stores in, and other household adjuncts, were the first to be examined, and the sepoys did their work thoroughly, thrusting their bayonets down in all directions, so that had a living person been concealed there, he must inevitably have been slain. These having provided no result, they proceeded to break open all the provision cases, wine cases and bins, wrecking every article that could possibly have provided shelter for a human being; but, owing to the fact that the circle of light thrown by their single torch was limited, the true dimensions of the cellar had not yet been discovered, and it was becoming evident that the sepoy leader did not believe that his prey was any longer in the building, and that he was getting anxious to be off. There were still so many houses remaining to be looted—houses where they could sate their blood-lust on helpless men, women, and children—that it seemed a pity to waste any more time where they were.

This fact, Chaloner gathered from his limited knowledge of Ûrdu, the man mentioned to his followers, and the diversion occurred in the very nick of time, for the sepoy who carried the torch was making his way toward that part of the cellar from which the light would probably have betrayed the fugitives' hiding-place.

He paused just at the critical moment, hesitated, as though loath to leave the task unfinished—he was, it afterwards transpired, the brother of the sepoy whom Shere Singh had killed—and then avarice overcame his desire for revenge. He turned and joined his companions, and the next moment Chaloner heard them clattering off up the stairs in their heavy ammunition-boots. Never had anything sounded sweeter in his ears, for he knew that their awful danger was past, for the time being at least, and that they were safe for a little while longer. A little later the three cramped and impatient fugitives heard the sepoys leave, by way of the garden this time, and then they crawled slowly and painfully from the hiding-place which had served their purpose so well, and, sitting on the bottom step of the cellar, debated together upon their next move.

"The only thing for us to do is to try to reach the fort, if Shere Singh knows where that is," remarked Chaloner; "for only there do I believe that we shall now find any British soldiers. Those in charge of the various guards, gates, and bastions must by this time either have fled the city or have gathered at some known rendezvous. That rendezvous can scarcely be anywhere else than at the fort, it being the only place, so far as I know, where they could hold out. What say you, Subâhdar Sahib?"

"That also is my opinion, *Huzoor*," answered Shere Singh, "and I advise that we make for that place as soon as we can. It is at the end of the Chandni Chauk, and not more than three-quarters of a mile from where we are now. It is quite dark by this time, surely, and we shall be reasonably safe in venturing out. But, sahibs, we must *not* be seen again in these uniforms. It seems that we have somehow been discovered, though how they should come to imagine that we slew that sepoy upstairs I do not know. It would appear that, since we arrived this morning, and were recognized by that mob near the Kashmir Gate, we have been searched for throughout the city. Perhaps they may, after all, have caught a glimpse of us at the telegraph office, and have seen us come this way. At any rate we dare not risk wearing these clothes any longer, and if ye will wait here I will try to get other disguises in which we shall be safe. There will be plenty of native garments in the servants' quarters at the end of the garden; and, as we know, the servants have deserted long ago. If the Presence will spare me, I will go and get those clothes of which I speak." And before Chaloner could utter a word by way of protest, Shere Singh had risen to his feet and disappeared like a shadow.

CHAPTER VI

They Blow up the Magazine

WHEN the Subâhdar padded down the cellar steps again with his accustomed stealthy tread, looking like a great grey ghost in the dim light of the fragment of torch which they had lighted, the others saw that he held in his arms a great bundle of clothing, beneath which he was nearly smothered. He must have looted every available garment.

"Truly our *ikbâl* (good fortune) is great, *Huzoors*," he exclaimed, with one of his rare smiles. "I have got just what I wanted, and when we have changed into these clothes I think we shall be safe, even in broad daylight. It is quite dark now, sahibs."

With these words he dropped the pile on to the cellar floor, and kicked the heap abroad with his foot, while Chaloner stuck the piece of torch into a convenient hole in the cellar stairs.

"See, sahibs," exclaimed Shere Singh, "here are garments of every kind; ye may take your choice. Here are the white robe and green turban of a holy man—how it got into the servants' quarters I know not; here are the white tunic and trousers of the *khansaman* (butler), with a red silk turban; and here are several silk *bûrkhas* (shapeless robes), if either of ye would care to disguise as a woman. This one is about your size, Fairbanks Sahib," he went on, holding up a beautiful amaranth-coloured garment, evidently once the property of one of the superior servants of the Collector's household.

"Then use it yourself, Subâhdar Sahib," retorted Fairbanks. "With those huge limbs and that bulky body of thine, thou wouldst make a fine woman."

"Perhaps we had better discard the women's garments," observed Shere Singh hastily, to whom the suggestion did not at all appeal. "What say you, Chaloner Sahib, to wearing this robe of the *gosain* (holy man)? Fairbanks Sahib and I could be thy disciples; and we should all three have but recently arrived from Ajmere. I suggest the disguise of holy man for thee, sahib, because—forgive me—of thy lack of knowledge of Ûrdu; the *gosain* is never addressed unless he himself speaks—he is too holy—and that will be a great protection for thee. Also for us; as no one, not even a drunken Pandy, would be bold enough to stop or question a *gosain* and his attendant *fakirs*. Thou mightest even attempt the rôle of a *Yogi*" (a very advanced sect of holy men, who are credited with supernatural powers), "if thou but knew some—what call ye them?—magic work."

"Oh! conjuring tricks, you mean," said Chaloner. "Well, as it happens, I am supposed to be rather good at that sort of thing; so, if you think we can carry the affair through, I do not mind being a *gosain*, or a *Yogi* either, for that matter."

"Then, sahib, let us agree each to take the part I suggest. Thou wilt be the holy man, and wilt never speak, save in a low voice to thy faithful disciples, Fairbanks Sahib and me, who will answer all questions, if any should be asked, or if we should be prayed to give an example of our powers of healing. Thou wilt have naught to do save to look as serious and preoccupied as possible, and we will give you the—what call ye it?—ah! the 'tip', when it becomes advisable for thee to perform thy magic. Now, sahibs," the Subâhdar continued, "let us get to work at once, for I would fain sleep this night in safety, and it is full time for us to be gone."

With these words Shere Singh proceeded to divest himself of his cavalry uniform, an example immediately followed by the two Englishmen, and in a quarter of an hour the three stood up in their new disguises, so altered that even their own mothers would never have recognized them. Chaloner, as arranged, wore the white robe and green turban of the *gosain*, while Shere Singh and Fairbanks had selected two dun-coloured *chogahs*, or mantles, to wear over their only other garments, a pair of loose white drawers and a kind of cotton singlet without sleeves. Their turbans consisted of lengths of yellow cotton material, swathed round their heads by the deft fingers of Shere Singh, while for foot covering each wore a pair of sandals made from the skin of the *sambuhr* deer fastened to the foot by thin thongs of raw hide. These, the Subâhdar explained, they would find rather trying because of their thinness, affording very little protection to the sole of the foot from the rough roads; but he declared that they would soon become accustomed to the discomfort, as he could vouch for from experience.

The change having been accomplished, they thrust their discarded uniforms away in the recess beneath the cellar stairs in which they themselves had hidden, while Shere Singh returned the garments from which they had made a selection, to the servants' quarters whence they had been taken. Their swords they decided to retain, since without them, in the rather unlikely event of their disguises being penetrated, they would be absolutely defenceless; and they contrived to conceal them under their cloaks by the simple process of slinging the sword-belts over their shoulders instead of round their waists. Then they were ready.

"Well," said Chaloner, standing up and shaking himself comfortably into his unaccustomed garments, "the *gosain* is ready. How about the *fakirs*; are they prepared to start?"

"This *fakir* is, at any rate," replied Fairbanks, and Shere Singh nodded assent.

"Then lead the way, Subâhdar Sahib," ordered Chaloner. "I do not know where the Chandni Chauk lies."

"'Tis not far from here, sahib," answered Shere Singh; "but it will not be correct for me, a *fakir*, to walk in front of the *gosain*. Thou must lead, *Huzoor*, but I will indicate to thee the directions in which to turn, speaking ever in a low tone. We shall be able to manage excellently in that way. And, remember, walk with thine eyes directed to the ground, as though wrapt in thought; so shalt thou the better escape penetration of thy disguise. And if by any chance we should be discovered, which I do not think likely, the only thing for us to do will be to out swords and die with our backs against the nearest wall. Fall not alive into the hands of the rebels under any circumstances, sahibs; your fate would be too dreadful to think of.

"And now," he concluded, "we must get away from this place; our lives are not safe for a moment while we remain. May Allah be with us and be our Guide! This way, sahibs; we will get into the streets by way of the garden. Beware lest anyone catch sight of thy white garments until we are safely among the crowd."

With this final caution Shere Singh piloted them through the darkness caused by the shadow of the building, and in a few minutes the trio found themselves safely at the lower end of the garden, just inside the gate giving on to the lane.

From the street which ran past the front of the house they could hear the deep hum of a dense throng passing and repassing, with now and again the shrill yell of some *bhang*-maddened fanatic, running *amok* among the mob; but although they listened carefully they caught no sound of life in the lane.

With infinite caution Shere Singh pulled the bolt back noiselessly—having taken the precaution to oil it while he had been away to fetch the disguises—and, opening the gate an inch at a time, peered forth into the moonlit alley.

The thoroughfare was apparently deserted, and at a low word from Shere Singh they filed, silently as shadows, out of the gate, which Chaloner fastened behind him. Then, quickening their pace, they proceeded sharply along the lane until they were at a safe distance from the house, and on the point of entering another and a broader street.

Here they adopted the formation suggested by Shere Singh, Chaloner going a little in front, his head bent as in meditation, with the other two a short two paces in the rear, their hands clasped in front of them; and thus they left the deserted alley, and in a moment found themselves moving eastward along another street, thronged with natives, but with no sign of a white face anywhere.

As Shere Singh had prophesied, Chaloner experienced no difficulty in making his way through the crowd, unhindered and unmolested. Everybody gave way before him, and nobody addressed a word to him, although a perfect battery of questions was fired at the attendant *fakirs*, who found it difficult to answer the enquiries and at the same time to keep pace with the *gosain*, who was striding along at a good round turn of speed. In his excitement and eagerness to avoid the horrible danger that hovered over them, he was unwittingly walking a good deal faster than was the custom with the usually slow-moving holy men, and Shere Singh was glad when an opportunity occurred that enabled him to offer a low-voiced word of warning. After that Chaloner pulled himself together and proceeded at a pace more in keeping with the character he had assumed.

They had been walking for about half an hour, Shere Singh and Fairbanks answering the rapid fire of questions with which they were being bombarded concerning the holy man, and Chaloner was beginning to think that they must be getting somewhere near their destination, when he was startled to hear a gasp of astonishment and dismay escape from the lips of the Subâhdar, close behind him, and he only restrained himself by a tremendous effort from turning to ask what was the matter.

Determined, however to learn the cause of Shere Singh's perturbation, he surveyed the people around with a stare which he strove to render detached and imperturbable; and well it was for him that he had his features thoroughly under control, for as he glanced up his eyes fell full upon the form of a tall man dressed in the uniform of his own regiment, the Fifth Cavalry! The man was walking in the same direction as themselves, and Chaloner instantly recognized him as being one of the four men whom they had overtaken on the jungle road during their ride from Mirapur to Delhi.

He was the fellow whose horse had been shot by the Subâhdar, and over whom they had ridden, believing him to be dead. He could only have been stunned, Chaloner told himself, and now, by all that was unlucky, here he was in Delhi walking along the Chandni Chauk, not two yards away from the men who had ridden him down. No wonder Shere Singh had gasped, for they were all three in the most deadly peril.

The fellow looked in their direction occasionally, but so far as Chaloner's furtive glances enabled him to tell, his suspicions had not yet been aroused; but should he happen to look more closely, while they were traversing a better-lighted portion of the street, perhaps, he could scarcely fail to observe the resemblance between their faces and those of the three *sowârs* who had slain his companions, for they would certainly be deeply impressed upon his memory.

And if once his suspicions should become aroused, he would surely attempt to verify them, *gosain* or no *gosain*; and a close inspection would reveal the fact that the holy man and one of his attendant *fakirs* had blue eyes, a feature possessed by no Hindu, and the game would be up!

He longed to be able to break into a run, to do anything to escape from the trooper's proximity; but his nerve held, and he was able to restrain himself from a course of action which must have been fatal. Besides, thank goodness! he could now see the fort, at the extreme end of the street, and he noticed that the crowd was beginning to thin out a good deal. They had evidently not yet screwed up their courage to the point of actually bearding the British Lion in his den, and seemed resolved to keep well out of range of the avenging rifles. Presently, too, to Chaloner's great relief, the *sowâr* turned off down a side street, without bestowing another glance in their direction, and they found themselves almost alone. One of the few remaining pedestrians, observing that the *gosain* was still heading in the direction of the fort. ventured on a timid word of warning to Shere Singh; but he replied shortly that the *gosain* feared neither *Farângi* nor anybody else, and that no harm would come to one with so holy a reputation as this man.

The would-be benefactor shrugged his shoulders, and himself turned down another street. He apparently did not consider the *gosain's* holiness powerful enough to protect anybody but the *gosain* himself, and was not taking any unnecessary risks.

A cautious glance rearward by Fairbanks showed that they were not being followed, and there was nobody near or in front of them. They therefore quickened their pace, and a few minutes later found themselves standing in the shadow of the fort of Delhi. They were safe at last, Chaloner assured himself.

Shere Singh, however, had had, for the past few minutes, his own ideas on the matter, though he forbore to mention them.

After a quick glance round, to make sure that they were not observed, the Subâhdar whipped his sword from under his cloak and gave a couple of resounding knocks with the hilt upon the iron-studded oaken door, and then stood ready to answer smartly the challenge which Chaloner confidently expected to follow.

Everything remained as still as the grave, however, and no answer came, although the other two followed the Subâhdar's example, and made clamour enough, one would have said, to raise the dead. This they continued for some five minutes, and were at length reluctantly obliged to come to the conclusion that the British had found themselves compelled to abandon the place.

The question that now presented itself was: "Where had the little garrison gone?"

Chaloner knew that the British portion of the garrison had been very small, the bulk of the fort forces being, as usual, composed of native regiments, the Fifty-seventh Native Infantry in this case; but it was evident that his countrymen had driven the mutineers out of Delhi fort before evacuating it themselves. The probability also was that they had destroyed the surplus arms kept there. The magazine itself was not situated inside the walls, but at a little distance from the fort; and, since there had been no explosion in the city since their arrival, they hoped that the magazine would still be in British hands. It was absolutely certain that if the British had been compelled to abandon it they would have first blown it up; and the inference therefore was that British troops would still be found there.

This surmise Chaloner forthwith communicated to his friends, and then discovered that Shere Singh had been afraid that the fort had been abandoned almost from the moment when he set eyes on it, consequent upon the fact that he had been unable to detect any sign of life about it. But he now heartily agreed with Chaloner that, if anywhere, they ought to find some British soldiers in the magazine, and the trio set out for the place without wasting any more time.

A few minutes' swift walk through side streets, during which they encountered no one, brought them within sight of the magazine, and they had scarcely halted before the gate when they were delighted to hear a challenge ring out, through the darkness, of: "Halt! who goes there?"

"Friends," replied Chaloner; "refugees from Mirapur. I am Lieutenant Peter Chaloner, of the Fifth Bengal Cavalry, and with me are the Subâhdar Shere Singh, of the same regiment, and Mr. Neville Fairbanks, of the Mirapur Telegraph Office. We are disguised, however, as a holy man and two *fakirs*."

There was the sound of a whispered colloquy inside the gate, and the trio heard the heavy footsteps of somebody running across the flagged courtyard, evidently taking a message from the sentry. Then the footfalls of a couple of men were heard returning, and presently a little observation-port in the gate itself was opened and the light of a lantern streamed through.

"So, two of you are officers and the third a clerk, eh?" exclaimed a cultivated voice. "Well, all I can say is, that you don't look it. Here, you," pointing to Chaloner, "come a little closer; the others stay where they are."

Chaloner approached, and saw that his questioner was a young man of about thirty years of age, dressed in the uniform of an English infantry lieutenant. He was looking pale and worried, yet there was a twinkle of humour in his eyes.

For a full minute he scrutinized Chaloner closely, then remarked: "All right, young 'un! you're English, I can see. Let him and his friends come in," he added to some unseen person.

The sally-port was opened, and the next instant the three fugitives stood safely inside the magazine. The young officer stepped up to Chaloner with the words: "You are welcome, sir, to what little we have to offer; but I am afraid you've only stepped out of the frying-pan into the fire if you expect to be safe here. Let me introduce myself, however. I am Lieutenant Alan Williamson, of the Forty-ninth—what's left of 'em. And this, I take it, is the Subâhdar, and this Mr. Fairbanks? Pleased to make your acquaintance, gentlemen, especially as I have only nine men with me here."

"*Nine!*" ejaculated Chaloner in amazement. "Then where on earth is the garrison of the fort, and all our men who were in Delhi?"

"The fort was abandoned this afternoon, Mr. Chaloner," was the reply, "and the garrison has been, and is being, utilized in trying to save the lives of the civilian population of Delhi. With Major Cowan in command, this small force is working through the European quarter, picking up all our people as it goes; and when this has been done it will either try to cut its way out and reach Mirapur, or wi'l entrench itself at the Ajmere or Delhi Gate, and endeavour to hold out until help comes. The fort is impossible to defend; there are no stores there, and the place is so ruinous it could be carried at the first assault. I, personally, have orders to hold this magazine to the last gasp; and if I cannot keep the enemy out, to—to see that they do not get the ammunition, at any rate. There you have the situation in a nutshell."

"I see what you mean," said Chaloner. "If you can't hold out, you'll blow up the place. Well, I can tell you that, if you are expecting relief from Mirapur, it won't arrive; so do not reckon on it." And he proceeded to describe the situation there, due to the senile inefficiency of Brigadier Hewlitt.

When he had finished, Williamson exclaimed: "Do you, then, mean to tell me that Brigadier Hewlitt has allowed himself, with that strong force of British troops at his disposal, to be overawed by a few regiments of mutinous sepoys?"

"Overawed is hardly the word," returned Chaloner. "But the old fellow cannot muster enough energy to act; all he wants is to be let alone, and not all the entreaties of his officers are sufficient to cause him to take action. Nor will he allow his subordinates to move. Things are just at a deadlock there, and nothing is to be expected from Mirapur."

"Then, Heaven help us here!" said Williamson solemnly. "Our men at one or other of the Gates are relying on speedy help, as I was here. But now—all that remains is for them to sell their lives as dearly as possible, in defence of the women and children.

They would find great difficulty in cutting their way through to Agra, or Allahabad, and Aligarh and Bareilly are in the hands of the mutineers. And as for me, all that seems left is to blow up this place. I expected to be attacked to-day, and an assault is certain to be delivered to-morrow. I cannot hope to hold the place, without relief, with only nine men."

"Twelve," corrected Chaloner.

"Twelve? Oh! I see; you mean you will help?" said Williamson. "Thanks very much, Chaloner! but I'm afraid the extra three will not make much difference, this place is so large. But I shall hang on as long as I can, you may be sure. And now you're all looking very tired—I suppose you haven't had much sleep since leaving Mirapur—so I suggest that you three turn in and get a good rest. You will need all your strength to-morrow, I promise you."

The three were only too glad to adopt the suggestion, and in less than five minutes after their heads touched their pillows in the cubicles assigned to them, they were fast asleep.

A shrill bugle call aroused them the next morning, to find that Williamson was already hard at work completing his preparations for defence. He had, as it happened, six 9-pounder field-pieces, and these he loaded to the muzzle with bullets, nails, and all sorts of odds and ends, rammed down on top of the solid round-shot. They were then placed in a row at the top of the long ramp leading up from the gate to the roof of the magazine, so that, when the gate was blown in, as it was sure to be, the cannon could sweep lanes through the ranks of the advancing sepoys. Chaloner and his two companions at once got their breakfast, and then set to work to assist with the preparations for defence.

While Williamson and his nine men were working on

the roof and the walls, our friends entered the magazine itself, and commenced beating in the heads of all the powder-casks, turning their contents on to the floor, breaking up and spilling abroad numberless packets of cartridges, among which they emptied more powder, and finally rolling as many casks of powder round the heap as they had time and strength for.

This finished, a good thick train of powder was laid away from the magazine, through the open door, terminating at the foot of a small tamarind tree growing at the top of the ramp. Then all spare muskets and other arms not actually in use by the defenders were collected and placed on top of the powder, so that they should be destroyed by the explosion, and not fall into the hands of the sepoys. By the time that all preparations were completed it was getting on for midday, and Williamson pronounced that they might expect to be attacked at any moment.

As a matter of fact, the words were scarcely out of his mouth before an uproar made itself heard in the distance, approaching nearer and nearer, until it resolved itself into the tramp of a large body of infantry; and a few minutes later a man in a resplendent uniform, mounted upon a gaily caparisoned horse, rode up to the gate and bade the garrison surrender, promising a safe conduct to Mirapur if the place were yielded up without a struggle.

For answer, Williamson pointed to the Union Jack floating above their heads, and laughed scornfully. The rider snarled something in Hindustani, uttered a sharp word of command to his men, and in a moment the air was vibrant with the discharge of artillery and musketry.

Each of Williamson's men had been provided with half a dozen loaded muskets, and a pile, also loaded, lay close at hand as an emergency supply, while one man was told off to reload the discharged weapons.

The first method of attack adopted by the mutineers consisted in attempting to carry the place by storm, using scaling-ladders; but as fast as the head of a sepoy appeared above the battlements, the top of the ladder was pushed outward and sent crashing into the ditch below, taking its living burden with it.

But as there were only twelve men to attend to all points of attack, it was obvious that the enemy had only to set up enough ladders to be certain of gaining a foothold somewhere; and, sure enough, when Chaloner glanced up, shortly after the commencement of the attack, he observed some sepoys clambering in over the parapet at a spot where there were no defenders.

Seizing his sword, and calling to Shere Singh, he rushed to the spot, and the two laid about them with such effect that, within a minute, the few of the enemy who had gained a foothold were either dead or had jumped headlong to the ground to escape those terrible blades. Their ladder was thrown down, and Chaloner and the Subâhdar turned just in time to observe a great flash of fire and a column of smoke from the gateway. The smoke cleared away slowly, revealing the stout oaken gate in splinters, and, outside, a body of sepoys drawn up, ready for the charge.

"Leave the walls!" shouted Williamson. "To the guns, for your lives; they're coming!"

And as the men sprang to obey, the first rank of the enemy gained the foot of the ramp and began to swarm up it, thick as bees, their bayonets flashing in the broiling sun.

Then, *Crash! crash! crash!* and yet again, *Crash! crash! crash!* roared the six field-guns, one after the other, and an iron storm tore through the sepoy ranks.

Cries, shrieks, and execrations arose on the still afternoon air, and as the smoke cleared away it could be seen how awful the execution had been. The ramp was strewn with dead and dying, and the defenders added to the carnage by repeated volleys from their muskets.

"Reload!" the order rang out; the guns were sponged out, fresh charges rammed home, and then:

"Look behind, sir!" shouted somebody.

Williamson looked, and saw that the end had come.

While he and his men had been serving the guns, another force had once more erected their ladders, and had reached the roof in overwhelming numbers. There was only one thing to do.

"Scully!" called the lieutenant.

"Ready, sir," replied a loud, firm voice.

Then Williamson raised his hand, and at the same moment Scully laid a lighted linstock to the end of the powder-train.

Chaloner saw a column of flame spring upward with an awful, whistling roar; there was a terrific concussion, as though the world were dissolving into its elements; a column of smoke leaped into the air to an enormous height, mingled with great fragments of masonry, broken muskets, pieces of powder barrels, aye, and the limbs of human beings, in the midst of which the very roof of the magazine seemed to heave itself up, to fall slowly back again in fragments.

Following the appalling roar of the explosion there came a silence as of the grave, while the enemy outside stood dumb and aghast at the catastrophe.

Then fragments of falling debris began to hurtle earthward, smiting down many more of the mutineers, and the spell was broken. The sepoys had carried the magazine, it is true, but their victory was fruitless; there was no longer a magazine to occupy; nor could there be seen any surviving Englishman upon whom to wreak their vengeance.

But in a little cavity below the ramp, one white man and three brown men were crouching unseen. One was Williamson, who had marvellously survived; the three brown men were our friends from Mirapur—all that were left of that gallant little garrison. The sepoys, disheartened by the loss of so many of their number for so negative a result, returned to the city, over which a huge mushroom-shaped cloud of smoke now hovered, like some dreadful omen of the horror that was in store for Delhi.

CHAPTER VII

Spies!

MILES away from Delhi the roar of the explosion of the magazine was heard, the shock felt; and a party of refugees, making their slow way toward safety—as they hoped—under guard of the pitiful remnant of the British garrison who had managed to escape from the city, turned at the sound and saw the black, mushroom-shaped cloud hanging like a pall over the domes and minarets behind them.

"Thank God!" ejaculated Major Cowan, who had at the last moment decided not to attempt to hold any position whatever in Delhi, but had resolved to endeavour, in spite of the difficulty, to convoy his precious charges safely to Agra, or some other place where there was known to be a strong British garrison—"Thank God! Williamson has blown up the magazine! I knew the brave fellow could not hope to hold out, and I only hope that he has sent a good number of those black fiends to Gehenna. It would have been a dreadful set-back to us if the Pandies had secured possession of all those arms and that ammunition; there was a sufficiency of both there to have equipped over again the whole native army. Well, he's gone, poor fellow, and his brave companions with him; but he has died a glorious death. I only hope that I may make as brave an end when my time comes."

Major Cowan was, however, not quite correct in his

conjecture that all the defenders of the magazine had perished, as we have seen.

At the last moment, when Scully was actually applying his linstock to the train, Williamson had dropped over the side of the ramp, our three friends following him, and they had dived into one of the little arches upon which the ramp was built, and which were used for various storage purposes, just as the spark reached the powder.

They had been nearly killed by the concussion, which at such close quarters was terrific, causing the blood actually to flow from nose and ears; but they had escaped the full fury of that tremendous blast, and, were, moreover, sheltered from falling fragments, which came hurtling earthward for several seconds afterwards. Scully, the man who had actually fired the train, had leaped for safety down the other side of the ramp; but he, poor fellow, had been killed by a mass of masonry; while as for the other white men, they had simply been blown to atoms. Williamson, Chaloner, Fairbanks, and Shere Singh were the sole survivors, and it was very fortunate for them that so many sepoys had likewise been slain by the explosion, while the remainder had been scared out of their wits; otherwise, had they mustered sufficient courage to search the ruins, they must inevitably have discovered the four refugees, and the latter would of course have been slaughtered on the spot.

"Now what do you three fellows intend to do next?" enquired Williamson, as they crouched down in the darkest corner of the ruined arch, where they had determined to wait until it became sufficiently dark to permit of traversing the streets in comparative safety.

"Well," returned Chaloner, "to be quite frank, I really don't know. We came here, in the first place, hoping to warn our people of the rising before the mutineers could arrive; but, unfortunately, we did not get through soon enough to be of any service. I suppose the proper thing would be for us to return to Mirapur to report; but I really do not see what good that would do. Shere Singh's and my own regiment is scattered to the winds by this time; and although I suppose I could exchange into some other corps at Mirapur, I do not feel much like going back there and remaining idle because of the Brigadier's extreme reluctance to make a move of any sort. To me it looks as though the troops there will be obliged to sit down and wait with folded arms until somebody goes up to supersede Hewlitt and start the men moving. He will never do so of his own accord, and as things are now there will probably be nothing doing there for weeks. No, the idea of going back to Mirapur certainly does not appeal to me. In any place except that, my friends and I might be of some use."

"I agree with you," returned Williamson; "and I may tell you that you are at this moment in the place, of all others, where you will be enabled to make yourselves of the greatest use to your country."

"What! Here, in Delhi?" exclaimed Chaloner.

"Yes," replied the lieutenant. "Let me explain. Delhi is at this moment in the hands of the mutineers, but it will not be allowed to remain so; we may be sure of that. As soon as the British troops are properly mobilized, and begin concerted action, Delhi, being a strategic point of immense importance, will be one of the first places, if not *the* first, to be attacked by us. Nothing can be done in this part of India until Delhi is again in British hands, and you may be sure that not many days will elapse before we shall have cur friends hammering away at these walls. Now, I need hardly tell you that when once our troops sit down to besiege this place, the one thing that will be of more value than anything else to our generals will be thoroughly complete and reliable information as to the state of the city's defences, the number of troops inside, the quantity of provisions they possess. In short, anything and everything that can be discovered regarding the resources of the mutineers in Delhi will be of enormous importance to our people, if that information can be conveyed to them. Such items as the points where the defences are weakest, where an assault might be delivered with success, would mean the saving of hundreds of British lives; might, indeed, make all the difference between their being able to recapture the city and being obliged to abandon the siege. Now, I am going to remain here, disguise myself, and immediately set about collecting information, so that I may have some news to communicate directly our troops arrive outside. Putting it bluntly, I am going to become a British spy in Delhi, and the best way in which you three can make yourselves useful is to become spies also."

"H'm!" said Chaloner. "Spying does not very strongly appeal to me. Yet I fully realize the truth of what you say. Correct information from inside, carried to our men outside, may make all the difference between success and failure, a long and a short siege; and I suppose Englishmen in Delhi are now so scarce that if we all became spies there would still be none too many to supply the information."

"You may take it from me, Chaloner," answered Williamson solemnly, "that we four are probably the only loyal men in the city at this moment. The rest are either killed or have already made their escape; although how they can expect to get away safely, with the whole country swarming with mutineers, is more than I can say."

"In that case, Peter," interrupted Fairbanks, "our duty seems plain enough. We must remain here and make ourselves useful by doing as Williamson suggests."

"Agreed!" said Chaloner, and Shere Singh also growled his acquiescence.

"And now," went on the lieutenant, "it is getting dark, and it is about time that we should think of finding some place where we can hide during the siege. It should be somewhere near the walls, and where the battlements are low: the first, that we may the more quickly reach the British lines; the second, that we may the more easily scale the walls, since that will be the only possible means of egress and ingress that I can at present think of. Then it will be necessary for us to lay in a stock of provisions, that we may be independent of others; for we shall have to make ourselves as inconspicuous as possible if we are to avoid suspicion and discovery."

"Shere Singh knows the city pretty well," said Chaloner, "and I dare say he can tell us exactly where to find the kind of place we want, unless you yourself, Williamson, happen to know of a suitable house."

"I'm afraid I don't," answered the lieutenant. "I have been here some time, certainly, but my duties have never carried me into the purlieus of Delhi, where I suppose we shall be safest in taking up our abode, since they are situated close underneath the walls."

"Very well then," said Chaloner, "we shall have to rely on you, Subâhdar Sahib. What do you suggest?"

"Why not again try the Collector Sahib's house?" suggested Shere Singh, after a pause of deep thought. "It is certainly not so close to the walls as it might be, but it is not very far from the Mori Bastion, where, as the sahib doubtless remembers, the battlements are low. That cellar is already well stocked with provisions, and there is our hiding-place under the stairs, which served us well yesterday."

"By Jove!" ejaculated Chaloner. "The very thing. That house should be fairly safe, since they have already searched it once and found nothing. I propose that we go there, eh, Fairbanks?"

"Just as you please, Peter," replied Fairbanks. "I imagine it will be as safe as any other place we could find. But if we're going I think we ought to be on the move before the streets begin to fill with the usual evening crowd. You see, Williamson's white face is rather likely to attract——"

"Why, of course," ejaculated Chaloner, smiting his chest. "I had clean forgotten my bottle of 'mixture'! I knew that the stain would wear off in time, so I put the flask in my pocket before leaving Mirapur, and slipped it into a fold of my turban when I changed at the Collector's. Here it is, Williamson; rub some on your 'phiz' and you'll be a darky like us in less than a pig's whisper."

The lieutenant, who had been wondering how he was to overcome the difficulty presented by his white face, seized the flask eagerly, and in a few minutes had anointed face, neck, hands, and arms with the liquid. Then, following the previous tactics of the others, he stripped the officer's facings from his uniform, until at the end of a quarter of an hour he could not have been distinguished from any of the other red-coated sepoys with whom the city now swarmed. It was agreed, however, that it would not do for him to be seen in the company of the *gosain* and the *fakirs*, so he decided to follow them at a distance of about a hundred yards, whence he could observe the direction they took and rejoin them when they reached the security of the dark alley behind the garden of the Collector's house.

In this order, therefore, they set out, and the short journey was completed without any untoward incident. Just as the moon rose, they found themselves once more standing in the lane, outside the garden gate of the Collector's house; and, so far as they could see, there were no signs that human foot had passed the threshold since their own on the previous evening, during which period so much had happened.

But they were by no means disposed to take unnecessary risks, and it was a very cautious quartette which, headed by Chaloner, slowly pushed open the gate and peered into the garden.

Chaloner was still carefully surveying the moonlit expanse before him for any sign of a lurking enemy, when the Subâhdar, who was last in the line, suddenly whispered:

"In the name of Allah, Chaloner Sahib, get inside quickly! There is somebody coming down the lane!"

He did not mention that the new-comer was wearing the grey uniform of a *sowâr*, nor that he shrewdly suspected he was the man they had encountered before, on their way to the fort; but he trusted that, as they were in the shadow of the wall, the fellow had not seen them. At any rate they would very soon know.

Chaloner sprang forward into the garden as though shot, with the other three close in the rear, while the Subâhdar softly closed the door behind them, and placed his shoulder against it. The lock was gone.

Shere Singh then reached silently under his cloak, and the next instant his long, keen *tulwâr* gleamed white in the moonlight. If the fellow had seen them, and was resolved to follow, Shere Singh also was resolved that it should be the last time that *sowâr* ever troubled any of them.

While the other three waited, on tenterhooks, just inside the gate, their drawn swords in their hands, Shere Singh peeped through the hole left by the broken lock, intent upon the verification of his suspicions; and as he waited he heard, to his astonishment, the sound of another man's footfalls, approaching from the direction from which they themselves had just come. He wondered whether, after all, they had been followed without their knowledge, or whether, by some unheard-of piece of bad luck, these two men had perhaps agreed to meet for some purpose in this very house or garden. If they had, he decided they must not be allowed to depart alive. Turning his head, he glanced at Chaloner, laid his finger to his lips as a sign for silence, and then whispered the single word "*Do!*" (Two!)

Chaloner understood, and passed the word to Fairbanks and Williamson, who placed themselves one on either side of the gate, ready to strike if necessary.

Then the footfalls of both men became louder, approached nearer and nearer, and, to the horror of the fugitives, stopped outside the gate.

Immediately ensued a low-voiced greeting in Ûrdu, and a short conversation which Fairbanks stored up in his memory for future use.

"*Salaam*, Chunder Lâl!" exclaimed the voice of the man whom Shere Singh believed to be the *sowâr*, and:

"*Salaam aleikûm*, Fuzl Aziz!" returned the other.

"Hast any news, Chunder Lâl?" questioned the voice of the first man, whom Shere Singh, now that the fellow's face was turned to the moonlight, saw was indeed the individual he had suspected him to be. "Hast heard aught of, or seen, the accursed *Farângis* whom I instructed thee to look for, and ever watch, when found?"

"None, Protector of the Poor," replied Chunder Lâl.

"I have searched diligently all day, but have not seen them; nor have I met any that have seen them. But the Presence may rest assured that they will not long remain undiscovered. I have told all my friends, and they have told their friends in turn; so that soon there will be hundreds watching for them. They cannot escape."

"It is well," growled Fuzl Aziz. "Now, Chunder Lâl, listen! Those three I must have, ere this week is out, or else thou shalt suffer for it. I have reasons for desiring them which do not concern thee, and they are strong ones. Besides, while they are at large in Delhi the safety of the Faithful is endangered; for the sons of *Sheitân* are cunning! So look to it that I have them in my hands soon."

"The Presence has no idea," enquired Chunder Lâl, in whining tones, "where they would be most likely to go, when they arrived here?"

"No, fool," growled Aziz. "If I had, should I have consulted thee, thou calf's head? I may tell thee, though, that I imagined they might have come here, to this house, and I had the place searched, but found them not. But someone *had* been there, some *Farângi*; for one of our men who returned to visit the house was found slain in it, his body hidden in a cupboard, by the men who came to look for him and for these *Farângi sûrs*. There was nobody here then, for they searched every corner; but they may return, so—keep thine eyes on this place."

"It shall be done, *Bahadur*," replied Chunder Lâl, "and I can promise thee that my spies will not let them escape. Does the Presence think it fitting that he and his servant should visit the house now? Perchance some *Farângi* may be in hiding there at this moment."

At these words Shere Singh stepped silently back from the gate and held his *tulwâr* ready. The other three held their breath and waited for Fuzl Aziz's reply.

"Not to-night, I think, Chunder Lâl," presently decided Aziz, after a lengthy pause for consideration. "The house has been watched all day, and no living thing has been seen to pass the threshold. No; do not waste thy time here, but see thy friends again, and bid them cease not a moment from their efforts. I am all impatience to get those men into my hands."

"The Presence shall be obeyed," replied Chunder Lâl humbly. "Has thy servant permission to depart?"

"Go in peace," answered Fuzl Aziz in a tone which hardly agreed with his words, "and see that thou bring me news of thy success when next we meet."

Peeping through the lock again, Shere Singh saw Fuzl Aziz catch up his trailing scabbard with his left hand, contemptuously toss a small coin to Chunder Lâl with the other, and then stride haughtily away down the lane. Chunder Lâl waited until the footsteps of Aziz had died away, then, stooping, picked up the coin and viciously hurled it over the wall into the Collector's garden. Then he broke out into a perfect torrent of execrations against Fuzl Aziz, which made even the hardened Shere Singh shudder, and, turning away after one final sulphurous outburst, went back toward the main streets by the same way that he had come.

The four men just inside the garden breathed freely once again, and, silently sheathing their swords, picked their way cautiously across the dewy grass toward the house, all of them thinking deeply. Chaloner was thanking his stars that chance had put them in the way of learning the fearful dangers that evidently surrounded them on every hand; Shere Singh was wondering what hidden cause there was to account for the rancorous hatred with which Chunder

Lâl undoubtedly regarded Fuzl Aziz, and also how that hatred might be turned to good account; and Fairbanks was recalling that part of the conversation between the two Hindus which related to the close watch which was to be kept on the Collector's house, and turning over in his mind a little scheme which had just occurred to him, whereby he believed he might be able to bring that surveillance to an end. Lastly, Williamson was trying to recall, but without success, where, and under what circumstances, he had heard both Fuzl Aziz's and Chunder Lâl's voices before.

Reaching a clump of bushes that grew at the upper end of the lawn, they crouched for a few moments, carefully inspecting the house. They recollected the remark of Fuzl Aziz—that the place had been watched all day—and wished to make sure that none of the enemy were on the premises at that moment. By "watched all day", Aziz must have been referring to the front of the house, they assured themselves, for certainly nobody had been on guard at the back when they had arrived.

And as they carefully scrutinized the dark and sinister-looking back portion of the premises Chaloner suddenly gave a start and rubbed his eyes.

"Think you saw something?" enquired Fairbanks, who was lying at full length beside him, and had noticed the movement.

"Yes," replied Chaloner, "I did; or else it was my fancy. I'm almost certain I caught a glimpse of a flicker of light in that room where—where the bodies were. It was gone again in an instant, but I do not think I could have been mistaken."

"Well, if you saw it too that settles the matter," said Fairbanks, "for I thought I noticed something of the kind as we were coming up the garden; but it was such a tiny spark that I did not say anything about it, thinking it might be a firefly."

The two immediately mentioned the circumstance to the others; a short council of war was held, and it was decided that they should investigate the matter.

So, again drawing their swords, they left the shadow of the bushes, one by one, sprinted rapidly across the moonlit stretch of grass between them and the house, and noiselessly ascended the steps to the veranda.

Then Shere Singh pushed softly against the French window leading into the back room, and to his astonishment it yielded at his touch. He had, he remembered, fastened the catch behind him when they had left the house on the previous evening. He said nothing, however, but gripped his sword more firmly, and stepped, silently as a cat, over the threshold.

There was nobody in that room at any rate, he assured himself, after a careful scrutiny, and beckoned the others to follow.

Stealthily, in single file, the four men crept from the room to the passage leading to the cellar door, and presently Shere Singh softly turned the handle and commenced to descend the cellar stairs. Arrived at the bottom, he listened intently, and presently heard the unmistakable sound of someone breathing, over in the far corner of the cellar.

Groping in the dark for Chaloner's arm, he seized it in his iron grip, drew the lad toward him, and whispered to him to strike a light and then stand ready to dodge a possible bullet from the unseen man.

With fingers that trembled slightly, in spite of himself, Chaloner drew out his treasured little box, and everybody heard the rough "scrape" of the match on the sandpaper.

At the sound a distinctly audible gasp came from the corner of the cellar, followed by a shrill scream of terror as the match burst into flame, and the four men stood aghast at seeing the slender form of a white woman spring up from behind one of the provision cases, stretching out her arms to them in entreaty.

She was quite young, evidently not more than twenty, but her dress was torn and soiled, her uncoiled hair straggled over her shoulders, and in her eyes was an expression of mortal terror.

She managed to stammer out a few words in Ûrdu, begging the supposed mutineers to spare her life, and then her tongue failed her, and she leant against the cellar wall, trembling with fright

Fairbanks was the first to recover his presence of mind, and he immediately began to speak rapidly to her in English, assuring her that they were not sepoys, as they appeared, but friends, who would gladly defend her with their own lives.

At first the poor girl seemed incapable of understanding what he was saying; but presently the sound of the old familiar tongue banished the terror inspired by the brown, fierce-looking faces, and she began to comprehend that these men were not what they appeared to be, but English gentlemen, fugitives like herself. The tall figure of Shere Singh she appeared to have entirely forgotten.

Presently: "Then you are really Englishmen?" she exclaimed. "Oh, thank God! thank God! In my terrible despair I had been praying for help, but when I saw you all standing there, with your swords drawn, I felt sure that Heaven was about to put an end to my troubles in death. Oh, gentlemen, you cannot imagine what a relief your presence is to me! Ever since late last night I have been hiding in this dreadful house, without food or water, expecting every moment to be my last; until I think, if it had continued much longer, I must have gone mad."

"Poor girl! poor girl!" exclaimed Chaloner softly. Then aloud: "Well, madam," he said, "the position of every white person in Delhi—and very few of them there are—is at the present moment more than precarious, and will become worse still as time goes on. But this I can promise you, that while these gentlemen and I remain alive, our swords shall stand between you and danger. The best thing we can do for you, however, is to see if we cannot think of some way by which we can smuggle you out of the city and back to the arms of your friends. Existence here is perilous in the extreme."

He then proceeded to make known to her his own name and those of his three companions; receiving in return the information that she was Miss Alice Graham, actually one of the daughters of the Collector himself. She had providentially escaped the massacre which had overtaken her family, by being at the time on a visit to some friends, and had returned home to find all her relations slain. The shock had of course been terrible, and she had been crouching, like some terrified wild thing, in the cellar for nearly twenty-four hours, having apparently returned very shortly after Chaloner and his friends had left on the previous evening.

It was, perhaps, fortunate that she had been so terrified as to remain hidden; for had she moved about the house in daylight she must certainly have been observed by the spies who had been watching the place all day.

As soon as the girl had recovered her self-control, and dried her tears, Chaloner searched for their old stump of torch, which had been left in the crevice of the stairs, and lighted it. He then sent Shere Singh to the garden to collect some fruit, directed Fairbanks to search for water, and assisted Williamson to prepare a fairly comfortable couch upon which Miss Graham could lie down and rest.

By the time that they had arranged this to their satisfaction, and had persuaded the exhausted girl to allow them to make her as comfortable as they could, the other two had returned, having succeeded in their quest. The five of them then proceeded to partake of a much-needed meal, discussing in low tones, meanwhile, the best method of getting Miss Graham safely out of the city; for they were all agreed that matters were in far too dangerous a state in Delhi to render it at all advisable for them to try to keep her concealed within its walls.

CHAPTER VIII

Hoodwinking the Enemy

THE meal at an end, Miss Graham was induced to stretch her weary body upon the extemporized couch; and so utterly exhausted was she that, having done so, she was soon asleep.

And as she slept, the four men in the cellar crouched together, continuing in low tones the discussion of various plans for the conveyance of the unfortunate girl to a place of safety. The problem bristled with difficulties, but at length Williamson evolved a scheme which, after weighing the pros and cons of it, seemed to promise a reasonable prospect of success. It would of course be necessary to obtain Miss Graham's sanction to the proposed scheme, but in view of the awful perils which threatened every moment of her stay in the city they did not doubt their ability to win her assent; and having agreed to submit the proposal to her so soon as she should awake, they proceeded to arrange for their own repose, and soon everybody was asleep excepting Chaloner, who undertook to keep the first watch.

Happily for them all, the night passed uneventfully; there were no alarms, false or otherwise, and when Williamson aroused the sleepers, about eight o'clock on the following morning, they all arose like giants refreshed.

Over a breakfast of fruit, Williamson unfolded to Miss Graham the plan which he had evolved overnight for her removal from the city; and in such vivid colours did they all paint the dangers which beset her where she was that they soon won her acquiescence.

Briefly, the proposal was that Williamson—who spoke the vernacular like a native—and Miss Graham, suitably disguised of course, should impersonate a Mohammedan bridegroom and bride proceeding to Gargaon, some twenty miles south-west of Delhi, to which place the groom was conveying his bride in view of the possible siege of the city by the hated *Farângis*. The task would be both difficult and dangerous, but the very audacity of it might win success, and failure could not involve them in worse perils than those which every moment beset them in Delhi.

To carry out the scheme correctly in all its details two assistants were required, one to play the part of priest and walk beside the bridal vehicle until it should reach the open country, to serve as escort for the bride and protect her from the jests of the ribald; and the other to procure the vehicle and ensure that it should be available at the proper moment. It is of course customary for the bride to enter the vehicle from the house in which the wedding ceremony is performed, and as in the present instance there was no such house, this presented an added difficulty; but Williamson's fertile brain foresaw this and was able to devise a way out. Fairbanks, who spoke Ûrdu perfectly, was to go forth into the city, hire the most suitable vehicle he could procure, and, impersonating the driver, was to be in a certain street at a given moment, where the bridal party were to join him, such an unusual procedure to be explained, in the event of awkward questions being asked, by Fairbanks's pretence that he had forgotten the address at which he was to pick up the bride and bridegroom.

In accordance with this arrangement, Fairbanks

cautiously sallied forth, and, watching his opportunity, at length succeeded in eluding the watchers and effecting his escape, undetected, into the streets.

Meanwhile Chaloner's bottle of brown stain was again requisitioned, enough of the stain luckily remaining to enable Miss Graham to colour her face, neck, hands, and arms. Recourse was then once more had to the pile of clothing in the servants' quarters, from which the lady succeeded in extemporizing a costume which would enable her to pass muster fairly well as a Mohammedan bride of the poorer class—the better, perhaps, as it is the custom for the Mohammedan women to go always closely veiled when appearing in public.

Having allowed Fairbanks ample time to secure the vehicle, Shere Singh, acting with infinite caution, reconnoitred the lane at the bottom of the garden, and, waiting until it was for the moment empty, signalled to the other three, who instantly effected a rapid exit, the Subâhdar, who was remaining behind, closing and bolting the door behind them.

With Miss Graham walking between the two Englishmen the party rapidly made its way out of the lane and plunged into the more crowded streets, heading for that in which it had been arranged for Fairbanks to meet them. As was inevitable, they were greeted here and there with jests and chaff from more or less intoxicated passers-by—for every liquor shop in the city had by this time been plundered—but it was not until they reached the street in which they expected to meet Fairbanks that they first encountered any sign of suspicion. The street was crowded with people, who, as ill-luck would have it, had assembled there to watch the passage of a procession in honour of Hanumân, the Monkey God, and, despite all their efforts to proceed, the trio were at length brought to a halt by the passage of the procession.

It was while this was happening that Chaloner—who was enacting the part of a *Hadji*—became aware of a disturbance immediately opposite him, across the street, and, looking more closely, perceived that it was caused by the determined efforts of a tall man to force his way to the front. The fellow's eyes were fixed intently upon the trio, and with a thrill of horror Chaloner at once recognized him as Chunder Lâl, the man who had been ordered by Fuzl Aziz to find and arrest the two Englishmen and Shere Singh. Luckily, Chunder Lâl had never actually seen either of the men for whom he had been instructed to watch, and was obliged to rely entirely upon Fuzl Aziz's description of them; but to Chaloner it appeared that he was regarding the party with a gaze of keen suspicion. True, neither of the trio answered in the slightest degree to the description of the gigantic Subâhdar, while one of them was undoubtedly a woman; and these circumstances seemed to confuse the spy somewhat, a fact of which Chaloner took advantage the instant the procession had passed and the party was able to resume its way.

A minute later they sighted Fairbanks lumbering along in a bullock *bylie* (cart), and glancing eagerly right and left, as though in search of someone. Chunder Lâl was close behind; therefore, with an angry shout, Williamson hailed the driver in fluent Ûrdu, asking wrathfully why he had not called at the house for him and his bride, as he had agreed to do.

Himself catching sight of the spy, and deftly taking up his cue, Fairbanks gave the agreed explanation, adding, on his own account, that the procession had delayed him.

Williamson professed to be satisfied, bade Fairbanks get down, handed him some coins, and, placing his "wife" in the cart, helped the "*Hadji*" to a seat by her side; after which he stationed himself at the bullock's head.

Fairbanks, seeing how matters stood, started to stroll slowly away, hoping to lure Chunder Lâl after him; but that individual evidently considered three better worth holding than one. He now stepped up to Williamson, the supposed sepoy, and touched him on the shoulder, while Chaloner and Miss Graham held their breath in suspense.

"Whither goest thou, brother?" enquired the spy softly. "Is this a time for marrying and giving in marriage, when all true men are banded and working together to sweep the accursed *Farângis* into the sea? Dost think that thy regiment can spare any man, even to the arms of a bride, when it is daily expected that Delhi will be surrounded and besieged by those whom we have sworn to exterminate?"

"Nay, brother, thou doest me wrong," replied Williamson. "I do not desert my post. I am but taking my bride to my father's home, at Gargaon, so that she may be safe from the *Farângis*; and I am returning to Delhi immediately that I have done so. Be not wroth with thy servant," he went on, pretending to mistake Chunder Lâl for somebody in authority; "I have permission from my officer, and shall be back ere to-morrow's sun sets."

Chunder Lâl's eyes gleamed as he listened to the glib recital, and he nodded gently as Williamson completed each sentence. Chaloner did not at all like the look of things.

The spy continued his questioning in a curiously silky tone: "And when wast thou married to this woman, O son of battles?"

"To-day, brother," replied Williamson, unaware of the trap that Chunder Lâl was setting..

"To-day!" exclaimed Chunder Lâl, as though in

horror and surprise. "Knowest thou not, fool, that to-day is the feast of Hanumân, and that on this day no man may marry or give in marriage? Knowest thou not the law, I say?"

Williamson's cheeks turned pale under their dye as he saw, too late, the pit into which he had been drawn, and Chaloner's hand stole to his sword-hilt. If they were to be denounced by this man, Chunder Lâl should not live to reap the benefit of his evil deed.

And then, in a flash, there occurred to Williamson a saving idea, just at the moment when all seemed lost.

"I know," said he, "that a Hindu may not marry on the feast of Hanumân (as a matter of fact he did not know anything of the sort); but I am no Hindu. I am a Mohammedan, of the faith of the Prophet, on whom be peace! With me is the Hadji—there he sits—who performed the ceremony. And"—putting everything on one bold throw—"who art thou that thou darest question a Mohammedan sepoy as to his actions? Begone, lest you kindle my wrath, and evil befall ye."

It was enough. Williamson's evident anger, his perfect command of the vernacular, had had their effect. Chunder Lâl had nothing to reply, if this man were indeed a son of the Prophet, since Hindu laws could not bind him. And so, although his suspicions were by no means disarmed, there was nothing else for him to do but to take himself off, which he rapidly did, having made up his mind to try to overtake Fairbanks.

Without waiting an instant, Williamson whipped up the bullock, and the *bylie* proceeded southward and eastward, toward the Ajmere Gate. They were saved for the moment, but there was no time to waste.

When Fairbanks turned his back upon the *bylie* he felt a little as though he were abandoning his friends in the moment of danger; but he knew that he would only increase the spy's already strong suspicions by remaining. He therefore glanced furtively behind him several times, as though afraid of pursuit, and from the fact that Chunder Lâl cast occasional suspicious looks after him, and was obviously a little uncertain in his own mind, he knew that it would not be long before the spy would follow and attempt to stop and question him also. As for Williamson, Fairbanks felt pretty certain that, with his splendid knowledge of the language, as well as of the native and his ways, the lieutenant would speedily find some means of throwing Chunder Lâl off the scent and sending him about his business; so he was not feeling very anxious as to the safety of his friends.

But he made up his mind that the spy should not be allowed to overtake him if he could help it; he therefore kept a wary eye behind him, and when he presently saw, in the distance, Williamson drive off in the bullock-cart, and Chunder Lâl begin to walk rapidly down the street in his direction, he thought it was time for him to do a little hurrying on his own account.

The spy evidently had him still in view, so, walking quickly along, and no longer looking behind him, Fairbanks waited until he came to the first cross-street, then turned sharply into it, and increased his speed as much as he dared without attracting attention. He would fain have run; but this would but have invited an immediate and general pursuit.

So excellent a pace did he set, however, that he was able to reach another street before Chunder Lâl arrived at the first corner; and, once safely hidden from the spy's eyes, he felt comparatively safe. He did not pause, however, until he had set so many turnings behind him that it became impossible for Chunder

Lâl to follow him; and then, not desiring to return to the house until the afternoon, when there were likely to be fewer people about, he lounged into one of the open-air wine-shops, or gardens, with which Delhi was plentifully besprinkled, and dropped into a seat at one of the tables, in the midst of a crowd of Hindus, Mohammedans, sepoys, and *sowârs*, in the hope of picking up some news. The terrible danger to which he was exposing himself by doing so never even occurred to him, and he ordered himself a cup of Indian coffee in a voice as firm as a rock, although he was surrounded by men who would have torn him limb from limb had they guessed the identity of the little brown-skinned man in the countryman's clothes sitting calmly in their midst.

For some time it was impossible to hear anything distinctly, so loud and incessant was the gabble of tongues, the rattle of glass and crockery, the shouting of men arguing or quarrelling; but, little by little, as his ears became more accustomed to the noise, he was able to pick out some fragments of conversation. One of these fragments interested him so greatly that he changed his seat and took up a new position, close behind two men who were leaning over a marble-topped table talking and gesticulating furiously.

As Fairbanks calmly seated himself at the table next to the two men, who were sepoys in the uniform of the Seventeenth Oudh Infantry, they turned round in their chairs and regarded him with an insolent stare, as though questioning how he, a mere countryman, a *ryot*, dared invade the privacy of two men of war such as themselves; and for a few moments it looked very much as though they meditated fastening a quarrel upon him. But Fairbanks feigned not to notice the savage scowls with which the sepoys favoured him, and, leaning back in his chair with a sigh of satisfaction, as though thoroughly wearied after a long journey, closed his eyes.

The men continued to regard him with hostile stares for a few moments longer, and then looked round to ascertain whether there were any other vacant places. But every table seemed to be in use; so, with a muttered execration on the apparently unconscious *ryot*, the sepoys, after a short pause, continued their conversation, this time in much lower tones, which taxed all Fairbanks's keenness of hearing to follow.

He sat there for fully half an hour, at the end of which time the two men called for their reckoning, paid, and departed. But that half-hour had been well spent, and Fairbanks had secured a good deal of very valuable information.

He learnt now, for certain, that Brigadier Hewlitt had no intention of leaving Mirapur, for any purpose whatever, without express orders from head-quarters; so no relief could be expected from there. Secondly, he learned that the King of Oudh had thrown off what slight allegiance he had ever paid to the British, and had allowed himself to be crowned, by the mutineers in Delhi, as the Great Mogul, the Emperor of both Hindu and Mohammedan India; that he had already massacred the few British families who had been unwise enough to take refuge from the mob in his palace, thus committing himself body and soul to the cause of the rebels; that the Begum, acting under instructions which she asserted she had received from the King, had ordered the city to be scoured from end to end for British fugitives, and that, when caught, those fugitives were to be slain; that a few families, and the remnant of the garrison, had managed to escape southward, and were supposed to be making for Agra, but that *sowârs* had been sent in pursuit, and expected to be able to overtake and slaughter them. Further, that the

King had issued a Proclamation calling upon the entire native army to rise and drive the British out of India; that the Rajah of Bithur, Nana Sahib, the darling of the *Farângis*, had revealed himself in his true colours and sided with the sepoys, determined to wipe out what he called the "slight" that had been put upon him; and also—the only piece of good news among the whole—that the accursed *Farângis* were said to be presently coming to besiege Delhi, and might be expected within a fortnight—as soon, that is to say, as they could bring their heavy siege-train up-country.

But this was not all. The young Englishman had also secured a good deal of exceedingly valuable information with regard to the arrangements which the mutineers were making to resist the coming siege, the number of men available for the defence of the city, and the amount of provisions contained therein.

The city, it appeared, contained thousands upon thousands of fighting-men; the soldiers were well supplied with munitions of war of every description; and there were provisions enough within the walls to last both garrison and population for several months, without stint. Truly, matters looked very black for the survival of British rule in India.

With spirits very much subdued by this unwelcome news, Fairbanks rose to his feet, and determined to attempt to make his way back to their hiding-place, so that he might talk matters over with the Subâhdar—for Chaloner could scarcely be expected back so soon. But, just as he was on the point of leaving the wine-garden, he heard the sounds of a body of cavalry approaching at a gallop, and he pressed forward a little to see what was happening.

He was just in time to see a squadron of *sowârs* sweep past; but he would have thought nothing more of the matter had he not happened to observe the persons who rode at the head of the troop. One, the squadron officer, was undoubtedly Fuzl Aziz; and the man riding on his bridle hand was no other than Chunder Lâl, the spy!

Seeing these two men together, at the head of a troop of cavalry, Fairbanks realized in a flash—or believed he did—what had happened.

Chunder Lâl, having lost sight of his quarry, had at once suspected Fairbanks of having dodged him of deliberate purpose, and this fact, added to his already strong suspicions as to the *bona fides* of the supposed sepoy and his bride, had caused him to become practically certain that those suspicions were only too well founded. Being therefore unable to overtake Fairbanks, and the others having, without doubt, long since gained the open country, the spy had run to his employer and related the facts to him, with the result that Fuzl Aziz had determined himself to look into the matter, and had gone at once in pursuit with a troop of cavalry, taking Chunder Lâl with him to identify the fugitives.

As he walked slowly back toward the Collector's house the young man's heart sank with a dismal sense of foreboding; for he knew that the heavy *bylie*, drawn by a slow-paced bullock, could not have gone so far but that a troop of cavalry would soon overtake it; and if that happened there would be no earthly hope, he knew, for the three English fugitives.

One thought of comfort alone remained to him —that there was, of course, always the possibility that the shrewd Williamson, put upon his guard by his encounter with Chunder Lâl, might anticipate pursuit, sooner or later, and devise some clever plan to baffle that pursuit; but Fairbanks was compelled to acknowledge that things looked very black indeed for the fugitives.

Shortly afterwards he reached the lane behind the Collector's house, and, finding it empty, slipped cautiously into the garden and sneaked up the lawn behind the various flowering shrubs and fruit-trees. Everything seemed exactly the same as when he had left the place a few hours previously; but nevertheless, he did not abate one jot of his caution. Slowly and stealthily he opened the veranda door, slipped inside, and then, making his way to the cellar, tapped twice in a peculiar fashion, giving the signal previously agreed upon.

To his delight he heard Shere Singh's voice asking who was there, and in a second he was beside the Subâhdar, eagerly recounting the day's events, and sharing his apprehensions with the old man.

The Subâhdar was naturally alarmed to hear that a troop of cavalry had been sent in pursuit; but he seemed satisfied that Williamson, or Chaloner, would find some way of outwitting them. What worried him more than anything else was to find that Fuzl Aziz and Chunder Lâl were so hot upon the scent; for he knew both men well by repute, and realized that, having got so far, they would not rest now until they had cleared up the mystery, and laid their hands upon the prey of which Fuzl Aziz seemed so anxious to possess himself.

They were still talking when a light tapping was heard on the cellar door, and in another moment Chaloner himself was with them, breathless, hot, and exhausted almost to the point of fainting.

It was not until he had had a copious draught of water to wash the dust out of his throat that he recovered sufficiently to answer their eager enquiries, and give them an account of what had happened since Fairbanks left him in the Street of Sweet Waters.

It appeared that directly after Chunder Lâl had turned away, unable to find an excuse for further questioning Williamson, but obviously still full of suspicion, the lieutenant had taken the bullock by the leading-cord and had continued his way toward the Ajmere Gate; being, much against his will, compelled to go slowly because of the crowd still remaining in the streets, and also that he might not attract undue attention.

As soon, however, as they began to approach the outskirts of the city, where the crowds were not so dense, Williamson increased his pace, and in a quarter of an hour found himself within a few hundred yards of the Ajmere Gate, though still out of sight of it. He now changed his direction, and hurried to the Delhi Gate, shrewdly surmising that, in the possible event of his being pursued, the people who had seen the conveyance making for the Ajmere Gate would naturally direct the pursuers thither; and, as several *bylies* were even then leaving that gate, after bringing in market produce, it was quite likely that the enemy might be thrown off the scent.

At the Delhi Gate very similar conditions prevailed, and no difficulty was experienced in passing the sentries, who, however, bandied a great deal of good-humoured jocularity with the supposed bridegroom. Williamson was, naturally, very much annoyed at this, as the sentries would be sure to remember the circumstance if questioned; and, once outside, he sent the bullock forward at its best pace, quickly outstripping the rest of the *bylies*, and soon found himself at a considerable distance from Delhi, practically alone on the broad, white Agra road.

But safety, he knew, was as yet far from them, and every moment he expected to see the cloud of dust on the road behind them which should indicate that the mutineers were in pursuit. He therefore eagerly discussed with Chaloner several plans for evading capture, speaking in a low voice, to avoid alarming Miss

Graham; and finally, between them, the two officers decided to drive on some distance farther, until they should have the road absolutely to themselves, when, at the first branch or cross-road reached, Williamson and the girl should dismount and follow it, trusting to the possibility of striking the main road again after dark. Meanwhile Chaloner was to remain in the *bylie*, drive straight ahead until the first signs of pursuit should appear, then himself get out, start the bullock running with a sharp blow of the whip, and hide beside the road while the pursuers swept past in pursuit of the empty cart.

They would, of course, soon overtake it, but, finding it empty, would be unable to determine at what point the occupants had left it, and would, it was hoped, abandon the chase. Chaloner would then watch his opportunity to leave his place of concealment and return to Delhi behind the baffled pursuers.

This arrangement at length decided upon, Williamson and Miss Graham dismounted at the next cross-road arrived at, and made off down the branch track at their best speed; while Chaloner, after carefully obliterating their footmarks from the dust, continued at an increased speed, starting the bullock at a sharp gallop now that the cart was so considerably lightened.

He succeeded in making a few extra miles before a cloud of dust, far away in his rear, warned him that he must dismount and abandon the *bylie* before the pursuers drew close enough to observe the manœuvre. He therefore watched for a suitable spot, which he found where the jungle bordering the road was comparatively thick, and then slipped out of the back of the cart, after giving the bullock a sharp cut with the whip.

The *bylie* clattered away, bumping and rolling from side to side, and Chaloner slipped stealthily into the jungle, where he crouched down, anxiously peering out through the thick foliage.

Ten minutes later he heard the thunder of horses' hoofs, and knew that the *sowârs* had swallowed the bait; and presently he saw them sweep past, with Fuzl Aziz and Chunder Lâl at their head.

The outraged bullock, which had probably seldom even trotted before, must have led the pursuers a considerable distance before they overtook the *bylie*, for more than half an hour elapsed before the men returned. Chaloner could hear them shouting and execrating among themselves some time before they actually appeared in sight; and as they passed, at a walk, it was evident from their remarks that they had no notion of where to look further, and were making their way back to Delhi, having given up the matter as a bad job. Fuzl Aziz, Chaloner noticed, was abusing Chunder Lâl at the top of his voice, probably for bringing them out on a hot and fruitless journey; while the spy himself was wearing an expression of scowling resentment that boded little good to his employer. Chaloner waited a little while in the jungle; then, after a cautious survey of the road, stole quickly from his hiding-place and made his way back toward Delhi at a fast walking-pace, eager to rejoin his comrades and tell them the outcome of the adventure.

He experienced no difficulty in re-entering the city and rejoining Fairbanks and Shere Singh.

A certain charnel-house odour, now strongly pervading the house, warned them that the time had arrived when they must get rid of the bodies upstairs if they proposed to continue the use of the building as a refuge; therefore, as dusk was rapidly falling, they decided to proceed at once with their sad and most disagreeable task.

Shere Singh found spades in an outhouse, and as soon as darkness had fully set in, and before the moon rose, the graves were hastily dug, the corpses—already in an advanced state of decomposition—were reverently placed in them, and the excavations filled in and covered up in such a manner that no trace discoverable from the street remained of the work which could betray them.

Discussing their plans together, at the end of a day when they had so narrowly escaped capture, they agreed that they would never again be seen all together, but would either work singly, or would take it in turns for two of them to go together while the third went alone. Thus, on one occasion, Shere Singh and Chaloner would join forces; on another, the Subâhdar and Fairbanks; and, to make a third change, Fairbanks and Chaloner; so that, thus ringing the changes, people whom they encountered would not be so likely to recognize them as all belonging to the one party.

In this manner, then, the three men perambulated the city, day after day, picking up information; and to many a queer spot and into many a tight corner did their quest lead them.

They frequented the low wine shops and *shalimar* (pleasure-gardens) where the mutineers were accustomed to congregate; they haunted the booths in the bazar, made friends with many of the sepoys in the fort —which the rebels had repaired after a fashion and strongly garrisoned—picked up chance items of news from the *nautch* girls who danced for the delectation of the soldiers; and on one occasion Chaloner in a moment of more than usually reckless courage contrived to penetrate even into the precincts of the palace of the King.

So the days crawled by, and lengthened into weeks, and still the eagerly awaited British force failed to arrive; while the mutineers, rendered daring by this seeming inaction, planned all sorts of impossible schemes, and pledged themselves to sweep the British out of India into the sea.

The King had established some sort of a Court in the palace, and had appointed Ministers to carry on his "Government", and officers to command his army; and although the Court was, of course, a mere farce, it happened that the old man had a keen eye for a soldier, and had managed to pick out all the best of the mutineer officers as his generals. And there were some really first-class, efficient men among them, who had added all that was best in the British military code to their own keenness of intellect and cunning, and their own ideas on warfare; so that, with the huge force which Delhi contained at their command, it began to look to Chaloner as though the recapture of the city was going to prove an exceedingly formidable task. All the more reason, therefore, he thought, for him and his friends to risk their lives every moment of the day, in order to secure information which would render that task the easier. And nobly they performed that duty too; for it is an unquestionable fact that, had it not been for the services rendered by that indefatigable trio, Delhi might never have been recaptured at all, and the whole course of the history of our Indian Empire might have been completely changed.

On a certain morning, when Chaloner and Shere Singh were making their way toward the bazar, Fairbanks having decided to spend the day at the fort with a sepoy whose acquaintance he had made, they noticed that the populace seemed to be in a state of greater excitement than usual, and that the soldiery, all fully accoutred, were making their way either toward the fort or toward the numerous gates in the city wall.

Of the first person who seemed to be in less of a hurry than the rest they enquired the reason; but before the man could reply, and as though in answer to their question, there came pealing through the air, from the north-west, softened by distance, the clear silvery notes of a British bugle, and the two men had to summon all their self-control to avoid betraying themselves on the spot by cheering.

For they knew the meaning of that sound. It meant that a part, at any rate, of the British siege-force had arrived overnight, and was now establishing its encampment on the Ridge, to the north-west of the city, that being the direction in which the bugle had been blown.

Fairbanks, conversing with his acquaintance the sepoy, a man named Ramasâmi, a Hindu, heard it too, and he also very nearly betrayed himself, so intense was his emotion as the familar sound thrilled through his every nerve.

Unable to restrain their curiosity, Shere Singh and Chaloner made their way to the battlements, scorning the manifest danger they ran of being stopped and asked awkward questions that they would not be able to answer; and upon their arrival there the sight that met their longing eyes was one that made them at once forget all the trials and dangers through which they had passed and were even then exposed to.

For up on the Ridge there had already risen a small town of white tents, while others were rising even as they watched. Away in the distance, so diminished as to resemble mere dots of paint, could also be seen the scarlet tunics and white sun-caps of the British soldiery, with here and there a splash of still more brilliant colour, which denoted the presence of a group of officers surveying the city walls through their field-glasses.

Wagons, carts, in fact every conceivable description of wheeled vehicle seemed to be there, the horses that had drawn them standing about, grazing on what little dried-up vegetation they could find; while hordes of white-clad *khidmutgars* and other camp-servants were to be seen busily unloading the teeming camp-equipment from the wagons.

But what thrilled the two servants of the Queen almost more than anything else was the sight of the squat ugly-looking seven-, nine-, and eighteen-pounder field-guns which, for the moment, had been drawn up in batteries, their black muzzles grinning threateningly at the city, their limbers and tumbrils drawn up behind them. Those guns would soon be knocking for admission at the gates of Delhi, and when once they got well to work——!

There was no sign of the big siege-cannon, nor of the elephant teams that drew them; but the two interested spectators knew that the lighter and more mobile portion of the army must necessarily outstrip the slower and heavier siege-train, and that they could hardly expect to see the *hâthis* toiling up the sand-hills with the big guns at their tails yet awhile.

For the present the sight spread out before them was joy enough; and, having gazed their fill, they turned and quietly made their way back to the streets.

As soon as they had regained the ground, Chaloner broke the silence with: "Well, Subâhdar Sahib, here they are at last—some of them; and the first thing we now have to do, so far as I can see, is to establish some means of communication with their camp, so that we can give them the information we have already secured, and keep them supplied with what more we can pick up in the future. And, to tell you the plain truth, I am a bit at a loss to know how we are going to manage it. There will be no more leaving the city by way of the gates, as we have been in the habit of doing."

"That is so, *Huzoor*," replied the old man; "and,

what is more, we shall not be able to go in and out by scaling the walls, as I at first thought might be possible. You may be sure that, with all these thousands of men to draw upon, the rebel officers will see to it that there is not a single *guj* (about a yard) of the ramparts left unprotected. So, since we cannot pass through the walls, nor climb over them, it seems to me that we must take the only other method possible, and pass under them."

"*Under* them, Subâhdar Sahib?" exclaimed Chaloner, looking at his companion in amazement. "*Under* them, do you say? Surely you must be joking! How on earth can we pass under?"

"We cannot do so at present, heaven-born," replied Shere Singh, "but that is no reason why we should not be able to do so in the near future. Listen to me, *Huzoor*. In order to be able to pass in and out of Delhi when we please, we must make a gate of our own. Now I know a place, not far from here, where the walls are not so thick as elsewhere. Why that is so I know not, but the fact remains; and there are some small houses, *Huzoor*, in that quarter, which are built with their backs right up against the wall itself, their fronts facing on a narrow street.

"It is a poor neighbourhood indeed, and only folk who are very poor stay there; in fact, one or two of the buildings have been fitted up as very cheap sorts of lodging-houses, where mule-drivers and pack-carriers, travelling *fakirs*, and their kind can buy a bed of straw and a meal of rice for a few annas.

"A few of these are empty, *Huzoor*; I saw them the other day, when I was down here with a man from the bazar. And my idea is that we should hire one of these, and, from the back room, construct a narrow tunnel, just big enough for one man to creep through, beneath the wall, having its opening, of course, on the other side. Fortunately, just outside the rampart, and immediately opposite the house which I have in mind, there is a dense clump of undergrowth and small trees, which will serve splendidly to hide the mouth of the passage where it comes to the surface of the ground; so that, if we are careful, we ought to be able to go back and forth as we please, unseen, taking care, of course, only to do so during the hours of darkness. What thinkest thou of my idea, *Huzoor*? Will it pass?"

"Surely it will, Subâhdar Sahib," replied Chaloner, "if we can carry it out. We will speak to Fairbanks Sahib about it; and if he agrees we will take the house, bring over our things—such as they are—the first dark night, and start in to dig as soon as possible. The sooner that tunnel is in working order the better I shall be pleased."

CHAPTER IX

The Secret Tunnel

WHEN they arrived back at the Collector's house they were fortunate enough to find that Fairbanks also had returned. To him Chaloner explained Shere Singh's plan for burrowing under the ramparts to communicate with the British camp; and the young man, after turning the proposal over in his mind for a few minutes, pronounced that, although exceedingly risky, it seemed the only plan likely to be at all successful. Accordingly the scheme was decided upon, the work to be commenced that very night.

Therefore, while the Subâhdar went off to negotiate for the renting of the house on which he had set his mind, the others, down in the cellar, collected a supply of such articles as they were likely to need—a supply of provisions, a basket or two, several spades, a garden fork, abstracted from the handy tool-shed, and a few other matters, tying them up in convenient-sized bundles, ready for transport as soon as darkness should render the operation reasonably safe.

Early in the afternoon Shere Singh returned, much pleased with himself, having secured the house for a couple of months for a very small sum—payable in advance—and no questions asked.

The moment that darkness fell, each man loaded himself with as much baggage as he could carry, they having made up their minds to take everything with them on the one trip; and in less than half an hour they were safely established in their new quarters, nobody, so far as they were aware, having seen them make the change or enter the house beside the ramparts.

The bundles were then unrolled, their contents stowed away, and then, the lantern having been lighted, they all betook themselves to one of the back rooms and arranged their plan of campaign. All working together, it did not take them very long to rip up half a dozen of the floor-boards, disclosing a space of hard-packed earth beneath, about five feet wide by some ten feet long, the latter dimensions being the breadth of the room.

It was conceded that Chaloner should have the honour of "digging the first sod", and so well did he work that the other two were kept busy carrying off the earth to another room in baskets, while, in addition, a heap of "spoil" was slowly accumulating beside the hole, which Fairbanks and Shere Singh were utterly unable to diminish, strive as they might.

Then, after an hour's hard work, Chaloner climbed out of the pit he had made, and took his place at a basket, Shere Singh descending into the hole to perform his share of the digging. And so it went on, turn and turn about, until daylight appeared, and all three were thoroughly fagged out. Then they replaced the floor-boards, locked the door of the room in which they had deposited the debris, and went above to sleep, enjoying the satisfaction of knowing that, even in one night, they had made a big impression upon their task, much more work having been done than they had imagined themselves capable of. Thereafter they regularly worked through the night, resting during the day.

They had been asleep but a short time, on the morning of the third day's occupation of the house, when all three were awakened with a violent start by hearing a dull, heavy crash, which sounded alarmingly near them, and they grasped their swords under the impression that all was discovered, and that their enemies were breaking in the door. But a second shock, occurring a few seconds afterwards, apprised them of the truth—the sound was the explosion of artillery in the British camp, and they knew that at last the bombardment of Delhi had commenced. The beginning of the end had come.

This was the sweetest music they had listened to for many a day, sweeter even than that of the silvery bugle-call which they had heard three mornings previously, and they returned to their couches to be lulled to sleep by the roar of the increasing cannonade as all the available guns were brought to bear, and the earth began literally to vibrate with the tremendous concussion of scores of guns firing at once. The idea that a shell might strike the rampart above their house and send the debris crashing down on the roof, crushing it and them to pieces, never occurred to them, or, if it did, they ignored the danger; and they slept soundly until late in the afternoon, when they arose and resumed work again.

By the end of the week the hole was finished, and it was decided that Chaloner should attempt his first journey to the British camp that very evening.

Accordingly, about nine o'clock, Chaloner prepared for his journey, and crawled, head-first, into the narrow tunnel, Shere Singh and Fairbanks carefully replacing the floor-boards behind him.

Having reached the outer entrance, Chaloner thrust out his head and gazed cautiously about him, but could see nothing except, very dimly, the dark blur of foliage which surrounded the tunnel mouth; and he therefore dragged himself right out on to the surface of the ground, finding, to his satisfaction, that the bush was high enough to conceal him even when he stood upright. He then cautiously pushed his way through the clump, rustling the foliage as little as possible, and found himself not a yard distant from the foot of the rampart, and exactly opposite a buttress, which would serve splendidly, he thought, as a landmark by which to find his way back to the hole, even in the dark.

Up above his head, as he crouched, listening, he could hear the regular footfalls of the sentries as they paced to and fro, and their occasional challenges as some individual passed on his way along the rampart. The moon was not yet up; there was therefore no danger of his being seen where he was; but the starlight, as is usual, was exceedingly brilliant, enabling him to make out the outline of the walls for some distance on either hand. Also, unfortunately, the light was strong enough to enable the sentries to see anyone who might attempt to pass across the open space between the walls and the camp, provided they were wideawake and watchful; and to Chaloner it began to look as though he stood a very excellent chance of being shot for his pains.

However, he was not going to give up thus early in the game, and he proceeded to make his way along the foot of the wall, keeping carefully in the shadow, in the hope that perhaps farther along there might be a larger amount of brushwood, through which he could crawl unseen until he reached a point far enough from the city to render him less visible to the riflemen on the ramparts.

His perseverance was rewarded.

About a couple of hundred yards north of the mouth of the tunnel Chaloner plunged suddenly down a slight declivity, upon which he came unawares, losing his footing half-way down, and finishing up on his back, in the midst of a thick tangle of bush which completely hid him from view of the battlements, over which a sentry, startled by the commotion, was leaning, his rifle barrel gleaming in the starlight as it rested, its owner's finger on the trigger, in one of the shallow gun embrasures.

Chaloner was a trifle shaken and dazed by his unexpected ten- or fifteen-foot tumble, and lay where he was for a few seconds, to recover his breath. It was fortunate for him that he did so, for as his senses returned he heard the voice of the sentinel up above call out to his neighbour:

"*Ai*, brother; didst hear or see anything below there, at the foot of the wall?"

"That did I," was the reply; "I heard somewhat, but saw naught, since I was not looking that way. What, think'st thou, was it? Surely none of these accursed *Farângis* yonder would be bold enough to come here spying beneath our very walls?"

"One cannot tell," replied the first sepoy. "They are fools enough, and brave enough for anything. That know I, for I once used to be *shikâri* to one of them, and there was naught that the harebrained *bândarwallah* did not dare. Many a time and oft did I wish him in Gehenna! Say, brother, it may have been an animal; or it may have been a sahib. Shall I fire and see what happens?"

"Aye, shoot!" replied the other sentry. "Perchance thou may'st hit something; and if the *havildar* (sergeant) comes, we can declare that we saw a sahib."

A loud report rent the still air, and Chaloner felt as though someone had slashed him across the forehead with a heavy whip. A second later something warm began to trickle down into his eyes, and he knew that the ball, fired at random, had been within an ace of scattering his brains. As it was, however, it had simply ripped the scalp, and he lay quite still, knowing that the second man's rifle had not yet spoken.

Then, after what seemed an eternity, he heard the two men growl to one another that there was nothing there, and the regular "tramp, tramp" began again.

Chaloner waited until the sounds told him that the men were at the other end of their beat, and then, rising to his feet, he plunged into the thicket that lined the bottom of the *nullah*, and was safely out of sight in an instant.

Up this *nullah*, or ditch, he proceeded until the thicket gave way to bare ground, and when he finally regained the level he found himself quite half-way between the city and the British camp, the lights of which glittered in the distance.

With a sigh of relief he brushed the blood from his eyes, and then picked up his heels and ran as hard as he could toward safety.

A few minutes' sharp sprint brought Chaloner to the edge of a broad, gravelled highway, and in an instant he knew where he was. He was on that branch of the Grand Trunk Road which ran from Azadpur and Karnâl and entered Delhi by way of the Kabul Gate; and he knew that, as it ran north-westward, he had only to continue along it to strike the right wing of the British besieging force. Immediately to his left was the Kishanganj Serai, a spot usually crowded with men and animals, but now standing ghostly silent and empty under the stars.

It was surprising, he told himself, that the British had not occupied the Serai with a strong force; for from its shelter it would have been possible to render the Kabul Gate untenable. And, that having once been accomplished, the task of destroying the gate or breaching the wall at that point would be comparatively easy.

However, he told himself, the British general no doubt had his reasons, and must know his own business better than Lieutenant Peter Chaloner could tell it him; so he gave no more thought to the matter, but, springing lightly from the bank into the road, proceeded to jog comfortably along, expecting every moment to be stopped by the challenge of a British sentinel.

And then he obtained the surprise of his life, and realized why no British force was occupying the Kishanganj Serai.

For, as he padded quietly along, his hide sandals making scarcely any sound on the thick dust of the road, he suddenly saw a figure detach itself from the shadow of the Serai and come running swiftly toward him, as though to intercept him; and Chaloner's keen eye at once observed that the fellow was carrying a musket, the barrel of which gleamed in the starlight. He also perceived that the man was wearing the red tunic, dark trousers, and high "pot" helmet of a sepoy!

"Good heavens!" he exclaimed to himself; "that's the reason, then. The Serai is a mutineer outpost, it seems, and a pretty-well-manned one, too, apparently, by the number of guns they've got planted there. Phew! I'm afraid I'm in a bit of a hole; for that fellow will be able to cut me off without a doubt!"

Chaloner's fears were well founded, for he had already run a long distance, had lost an appreciable quantity of blood, and was sadly out of breath, while the sepoy, running almost parallel to him, was of course fresh, and must inevitably head him off before he could reach the British lines.

Since, therefore, flight was out of the question, all that remained was either to fight or else trv to make the sepoy believe that he was one of themselves; a somewhat hazardous procedure, this last, since he was, although improved, anything but perfect in his knowledge of the vernacular.

Yes, there was nothing else for it. The man had gained the road ahead of him, and was now waiting in the middle of it for Chaloner to come up, his musket held at the "charge", and his forefinger curled round the trigger.

Luckily, he had evidently considered that he, with a loaded musket, was more than a match for any unarmed man, either *Farângi* or Hindu, and had not considered it worth while to raise an alarm. Perhaps he wished to have the honour of making a prisoner and taking him back to the Serai single-handed.

At any rate, there he stood; and Chaloner, seeing that a meeting was unavoidable, pulled up and walked forward very slowly, trying to recover his breath in readiness for the struggle that was inevitable.

When he arrived within half a dozen yards of the man the latter raised his rifle to his shoulder, and, pointing the weapon full at Chaloner's chest, bade him halt and explain who he was, what was his business, and where he was going.

Said Chaloner, who had been thinking hard during the past few seconds: "I am a man of the Thirty-fifth, and am taking a message to General Mehtab Singh, at Budli-Ki-Serai. I am not wearing my uniform because I shall have to pass close to the *Farângi* lines, and do not wish to be shot down by the sons of *Sheitân*. Let me pass, and quickly, brother; for the message is from the King, and admits of no delay."

And he commenced to walk toward the sepoy.

"Nay," exclaimed the latter sharply, still fingering the trigger, "come no closer, thou. Thy speech is not that of the Faithful, and I trust thee not. Come thou with me to our officer, Kâleh Khan, and show him thy message whereof thou speakest. If thou art a true man, and thy message genuine, he will let thee pass on thy way in safety. For my part—— If thou comest a step nearer I will shoot thee! Now turn, and precede me; and remember——"

"*Ai*, brother," interrupted Chaloner, forcing a laugh, "thou art overcareful! Surely thou canst recognize one of thine own brethren! And besides, my message is not on paper. His Majesty, on whom be peace! gave his servant instructions to bear his commands by word of mouth alone, and not to divulge those commands to anyone save the man for whom they are intended, the general Mehtab Singh. Therefore, I say, let me pass without more words, for I was bidden to hasten, and thou hast already delayed me overlong. Let me not have to explain to Mehtab Singh that thou wast the cause of my being late."

The sepoy lowered his rifle, but did not speak. He did not altogether believe Chaloner's tale, but at the same time he did not desire to get into trouble with the iron-fisted general, who was notorious for shooting his men—or officers—on the slightest provocation.

Meanwhile, seeing the rifle lowered, Chaloner pretended to believe that the man intended to let him pass, and before the fellow could again raise it to his shoulder the Englishman was within arm's length of him.

He raised the weapon and pushed the muzzle into Chaloner's chest, exclaiming: "Back, thou; back, I say! Didst not hear what I told thee?"

But before the man's finger could negotiate the strong pull of the Enfield trigger, Chaloner had dashed the barrel aside and grasped the man round the neck, putting out all his strength to hurl him to the ground. The sepoy dropped his weapon and strove to tear the Englishman's steel-like fingers from his throat, for

Chaloner was quickly choking the breath out of him; and, being a strong man, fighting for his very life, it looked for a few moments as though he might succeed.

Chaloner, however, was also fighting for life, for he knew that if once his grip slackened for an instant, and the man drew breath, he would call for help, and the entire sepoy picket occupying the Serai would at once be down on them.

He therefore strained every muscle to bring the struggle to a quick termination, and presently had the satisfaction of feeling the man's grip relaxing, as suffocation crept over him; and putting out every ounce of strength he had left, the Englishman placed his foot behind the sepoy's heels, and, thrusting strongly backward, hurled the man heavily to the ground, where he lay stunned and senseless.

Pausing only to possess himself of the fellow's musket, Chaloner darted away again, breathing heavily after his tremendous exertions, and presently had the satisfaction of losing sight of the Serai round a bend in the road. The sepoy still remained where he had fallen.

Feeling reasonably secure now, he moderated his pace to a walk, and was plodding steadily along when he was startled almost out of his senses by suddenly hearing the rattle of arms, immediately followed by a hoarse, loud shout of: "Halt! who goes there? Halt! or I fire!"

The familiar English tongue caused Chaloner's heart to leap with excitement, although he knew that the man's finger was already pressing the trigger, and a second or two elapsed before he could control his voice sufficiently to reply firmly: "A friend!"

"Advance, friend, and give the countersign," growled the sentry, who was rather disappointed at hearing the English words, for he had been picturing himself as the first man to give the alarm of a night attack, and the one to shoot down the enemy's leader.

"I do not know the word for the night," answered Chaloner, "for I am an Englishman just escaped from Delhi in disguise, after being there nearly a month. I have very important news, which must be given to the General at once, so you had better call your sergeant and I will get him to take me to his tent. By the way, who is the General in command here? My own name is Peter Chaloner, Lieutenant of the Fifth Bengal Cavalry."

"Why, confound me!" exclaimed the man, in surprise; "you surely ain't Mr. Chaloner, of Mirapur, got up in that *badmâsh's* rig? We all thought you were dead, sir; and I'm sure I should never have recognized you if you hadn't said who you were. Lucky thing you did, too," he chuckled; "for I was on the p'int of shootin' you first and inquirin' afterwards. We've had a lot of those *margallawallahs* (cut-throats) yonder trying to get into camp with sim'lar yarns. Yus, I'm glad you spoke; I shouldn't have liked to have killed yer. But you say you don't know who's in command? Why, Brigadier Mister-bloomin'-cautious Hewlitt, of course. That's why *we're* 'ere. We're nearly all Mirapur men 'ere, sir; barring a few loyal native companies, a few Punjâbi cavalry—who've got John Nicholson to lead 'em, however—and one or two more regiments, scraped together until the main force and the siege-train can come up. There ain't more than two to three thousand of us, all told; and the Brigadier, 'e's afraid of his life that the Sepoys'll come out of Delhi an' eat us all up before reinforcements can arrive. You ought to ha' heard General Nicholson a-tellin' of 'im orf the other day! You would ha'——"

"Yes, yes, my friend," interrupted Chaloner impatiently, "I shall hear all this later on; but now I must see the General, and give him my news. It's very important. So either let me pass or call the sergeant, quick!"

"Oh, I'll let ye pass, Mr. Chaloner, sir! I knows y'r face quite well now, in spite of y'r lookin' like one of them murderin' Pandies. No need to call the sergeant, sir. The word for the night is 'Lucknow'. Pass, sir, and all's well."

"Thanks, my man!" said Chaloner. "But first, tell me, whereabouts is the Brigadier's tent?"

"Yonder, sir," replied the soldier, pointing. "You'll easily recernize it because it's square in shape, and a bigger tent than any of the other officers have. Be sure that Hewlitt don't part with 'is little comforts, even in the field."

"Ah, I see it!" said Chaloner; "brilliantly lighted, too. That's a bit risky, seems to me; for there are plenty of guns in Delhi that would carry this distance. Well, goodbye! I may see you again later." And he made his way with quick, silent steps toward the tent, or rather pavilion, which had been pointed out to him as Brigadier Hewlitt's quarters, and, standing beside the open tent-flap, coughed loudly.

"Good heavens! what's that?" exclaimed a peevish voice from within. "There's somebody outside there. Go and see who it is, Baird-Smith, will you?"

Chaloner did not hear anybody moving, but the next moment he felt his shoulder gripped in a clutch of iron, and he was dragged roughly into the tent, the rifle which he had captured from the sepoy falling to the ground with a clatter.

"Well, of all the infernal cheek!" exclaimed his captor. "Why, sir, I'm hanged if we haven't caught one of those rascal Pandies in the very act of spying. Shall I call the guard, sir? The sooner we have the beggar shot the better."

"Stay a moment; stay a moment," interrupted a

huge-limbed, full-bearded man in the uniform of a general; "don't be too hasty, Smith. We may get some news out of him before we turn him over to the firing-party. Bring him here to me. I'll question him."

"All right, Nick!" replied the other officer; "do as you please, but keep your eye on him. They're tricky ruffians."

CHAPTER X

Buried Alive

DURING this colloquy, Chaloner, highly amused, had been scanning the faces of the officers assembled for the council of war—for such the meeting was—and was interested to find that he knew them nearly all. That coarse, fat man seated at the head of the table was Hewlitt, whom he had last seen at Mirapur. Beside him, on the right, was seated the handsome Neville Chamberlain, after whom Fairbanks had been named. On his left were Sir Henry Barnard, second in command, and Captain Reed, a most dashing Gurkha officer. The man who was still gripping his shoulder was Baird-Smith, the celebrated military engineer; and the big, bearded man could be no other than General John Nicholson, commanding the Punjâbi horse and the Pathan levies, a man already famed throughout India for his services on the north-west frontier, and who very shortly was to become world-famous, both through his instrumentality in capturing Delhi and by the glorious fashion of his death. A few short weeks, and that gallant figure would be fast turning to dust; but the terror and glory of his name endure to this day, when Indian mothers still quieten their babies by telling them that "Nikalseyn is coming"; when wild hill-chieftains still swear that they can hear "Nikalseyn's" war-horse trampling the earth, carrying on its back the ghost which has returned from the shades to see that the people over whom he used to rule while in the flesh are still obeying his precepts.

But Chaloner could foresee none of this, and his reverie was rudely broken by hearing the deep voice of John Nicholson bidding him approach.

He did so, his eyes sparkling with fun at the joke he was expecting to play; but he did not know Nicholson, he did not know that that wonderful man had already "sized him up" and was not in the least deceived by the disguise. Therefore he was much astonished when the General addressed him sternly with: "Well, sir, what explanation have you, an English officer, to offer for daring to appear before your superiors in that guise?"

The other officers gasped with surprise, and leaned forward, staring at Chaloner, while the latter felt his breath almost taken away by the suddenness of the attack. Not for long was he silent, however, and in a moment he began to pour forth his story, commencing from the time when he left Mirapur to carry the news of the rising to Delhi, and completing the account by relating his encounter with the sepoy outside the Kishanganj Serai. He gave full information of the enemy's dispositions inside the city, particulars of their defences, the number of men available, the length of time he thought they could stand a siege, and, what was most to the point, a description of the points at which an assault was most likely to be successful. He also mentioned the house under the ramparts, and the intention of himself and his friends to continue their work until the time should arrive for the grand assault itself to take place. Thus, he told them, it would be necessary for him to leave the camp fairly early, so as to regain the shelter of the house before dawn.

This account, to which every officer present, excepting perhaps the Brigadier, paid the utmost attention, lasted for over two hours, and when he had finished every man shook hands cordially with him, praised his and his companions' pluck, and thoroughly approved of the excellent work being continued.

"Young man," said Nicholson, placing a huge hand on the lad's shoulder, "you have done splendidly. We have sent several men into the city to secure the very information you have just given us, but they have not returned. They never will return now. This information is priceless, simply priceless, and I can promise you that your and your friends' services shall not be forgotten. I'll look after that. And now, Brigadier Hewlitt," he went on, turning to the General with an abrupt and unpleasing change of manner, "I presume that, after what you have just heard of the practicability of storming Delhi at not one but several points, you will no longer consider the advisability of giving up the siege at the very moment when your officers and your engineers have made every preparation for its capture?"

"General Nicholson," replied Hewlitt, flushing purple all over his fat, flabby, unwholesome-looking cheeks, "I very much resent your manner of addressing me. It is not becoming from so young an officer as yourself to one of my age and experience.

"Allow me to inform you, sir," he went on, "and you too, gentlemen, that in spite of our—ah—young friend's information, I am still of opinion that my present force is not nearly strong enough to attempt the capture of the city. And unless the reinforcements I have sent for arrive within the week, I shall carry out my original intention of retiring from before Delhi, and shall wait for some more favourable opportunity."

A hoarse murmur of disgust and disapproval, impossible to be restrained, made itself heard within the tent; and Chaloner felt his own cheeks flushing with shame for the cowardly old man whom a rotten system of promotion by seniority had placed in the position he now occupied, a position which could have been more worthily filled by the youngest and least-experienced of all the officers serving under him.

Neville Chamberlain was the next to speak.

"Sir," he said, "your officers have already informed you that trenches have been driven nearly up to the walls, mines have been run right under the ramparts in several places, and we have approached our batteries quite close to the battlements. Mr. Chaloner, here, corroborates the opinion of ourselves and the engineers, that breaches can be made in the defences at several points, and I am prepared personally to guarantee that another week or ten days of hard work will place us in a position to deliver an assault with the absolute certainty of success. Surely, sir, you will not be so—you will not nullify all our efforts, and put us back to where we began, by retreating at the very moment when a daring stroke would place us in possession of the city? Think of all it means to us, the capture of Delhi, and then ask yourself if you would be wise in retiring."

"All that you or your brother officers can say, Colonel Chamberlain," replied Hewlitt, "does not weigh with me one jot. I say the city cannot be taken and held with so small a force, and I shall not try. There's an end to it. I mean what I say."

"By heavens!" interjected Nicholson, his very beard bristling with fury; "that I, John Nicholson, should live to hear such a statement from the mouth of a British officer! I tell you, gentlemen," he went on, turning to the others, "if at the end of the week, when we are ready to do our duty and capture Delhi, any coward proposes that we shall give up the attempt and leave our task unfinished, I will pistol that coward, *whoever he may be, and no matter what his rank,* with my own hand.[1] I will be no party to such despicable, cowardly action, utterly lacking in everything becoming to an officer and a gentleman." And he fixed his fierce black eyes full on those of the apoplectic Hewlitt, while a murmur of approval and sympathy arose from the rest of the assembled officers.

"Sir! you—what do you mean, sir?" spluttered the Brigadier angrily, half rising from the depths of his Ceylon chair. "I would have you know——"

"I mean what I say, Brigadier Hewlitt," replied Nicholson sternly, "and if the cap fits, all I have to say is—well—wear it."

"By —, sir!" shouted Hewlitt, with an oath, now thoroughly aroused, "you go too far. I will not put up with that language from you or any man. Colonel Chamberlain, call the guard, and have General Nicholson put under arrest immediately."

"If you dare to do any such thing, sir," thundered Nicholson, advancing menacingly toward him, "I will see to it that——"

"Gentlemen, gentlemen," here interrupted the voice of Sir Henry Barnard, "pray recollect yourselves! This tent is no tavern, that we should use it for brawling in; nor is this the place or time for such feelings as are being displayed. If we wish for success we must all endeavour to stand together and work for the good of the cause. I am sure that Brigadier Hewlitt has no real intention of arresting General Nicholson—he is far too valuable a man. And I am equally sure that Nicholson meant nothing personal by his remarks, *with which I fully sympathize.* When the time comes, I feel certain that our efforts will not be permitted to have been made in vain, but that the Commander will

[1] This extraordinary remark is actually attributed to Nicholson by several who were present at the scene described.

allow his officers to attempt the capture of the city. Reserve your differences, gentlemen, for some other and more appropriate occasion, or, better still, forget them altogether."

And so the quarrel which threatened such disastrous results was temporarily patched up, and the appearance at least of peace resumed; but Chaloner could see that the sympathies of every man there, save Hewlitt, lay with Nicholson, and that there was nothing but utter contempt for the senile and useless Brigadier.

The short silence following was broken by Nicholson himself. "Mr. Chaloner," he said, holding out his hand, "we are all of us greatly indebted to you, to Mr. Fairbanks, and to Subâhdar Shere Singh. My advice to you is to go back now to your quarters in Delhi and to communicate with me—us—from time to time whenever you have news of importance. I expect that the assault will be delivered within fourteen days; but you had better leave the city, all of you, before the attack is actually made, and come into camp, to be on the safe side. For when once our men get inside, I can promise you they will show no quarter, and will not accept you for an Englishman, with that dark skin, simply because you speak English. There are lots of Hindus who speak English as well as you do, but that will not save them when once our people get to work with the bayonet. No, you must leave before we get in. And now you had better be off, as you haven't any too much time to spare before dawn, and it would be death to you to be discovered by daylight. You have done very well so far, young sir; I only hope you will continue your good work, and that luck will attend you always. Goodbye, and God bless you!"

With these words the great man again shook hands heartily, and Chaloner left the tent with a feeling that, for once at least in his life, he had seen and spoken with a *man*.

And now the hardest part of his task still lay before him; namely, to get back past the sepoy outposts undiscovered—for, for aught he knew, the picket at the Kishanganj Serai might be only one of many—and to reach the shelter of the brushwood around the mouth of the tunnel before day broke and revealed his presence beneath the ramparts.

Therefore, catching up the sepoy's musket, which he had dropped when seized by Baird-Smith, and assuring himself that it was loaded, he set off at a sharp trot in the direction of the sentry who had passed him through the lines several hours ago. The man was still there, but in the very act of being relieved, so he had no difficulty in passing out, his former friend standing sponsor for him; and a few seconds later, after a hearty "good night" to the two sentinels, Chaloner found himself once more on the Azadpur-Karnal road, which led into Delhi by way of the Kabul Gate.

Being, of course, now aware of the approximate position of the Kishanganj Serai, he took good care to leave the road again while still some distance away from it, and managed to steal past in the rear of the picket without being detected.

A quarter of an hour later he found himself, much to his satisfaction, at the head of the *nullah* along which he had travelled several hours earlier, and where he was, for the time being, comparatively safe from observation.

Fortunately for Chaloner, the sentries who had been guarding that part of the ramparts early in the evening were no longer there, and he therefore, without hesitation, broke cover and proceeded to make his way along the foot of the wall toward the buttress which marked the position of the mouth of the tunnel. Arrived there, he looked long and searchingly up at the battlements, and, seeing nobody there, dashed into the little *topi* (clump) of shrubs, and squatted down on the ground at the mouth of the tunnel to rest for a few moments.

Then, with a sigh of relief, he stretched himself flat on the ground, the captured musket still in his right hand, and commenced to work himself head foremost into the passage.

As he wriggled his way downward and forward he heard the sudden explosion of a gun from the direction of the British camp, and guessed that Nicholson was beginning the day by directing his fire on one or other of the weak places in the defences which Chaloner had described to him. He chuckled heartily, and worked himself forward another yard or two.

Just when another few seconds would have brought him to the inner end of the tunnel, there came a terrific concussion from somewhere apparently quite close at hand, and an instant later, with a horrible grinding, rattling noise, utterly indescribable, the walls and roof of the unsupported tunnel caved in on the top of him, crushing him flat to the earth. He was buried alive!

CHAPTER XI

Suspicion Aroused

FOR a few moments Chaloner failed to realize fully the extent of the calamity which had befallen him, being dazed by the utter horror of the situation.

Buried alive, and safety only a few short feet away! Why, had the tunnel been still open, he might, had he listened, almost have heard the voices of his friends in the front room of the little house; whereas now—now he might almost as well have been in his coffin.

It was, perhaps, this very horror of entombment that recalled to him his fast-wandering senses; he pulled himself together and at once began to consider whether matters were really as bad as they seemed. True, there was a crushing weight upon his body, which seemed as though it would press him right down into the earth; but there was a little air-space remaining just below his face, where his head and arms had prevented the earth from falling completely round him, and he even found that he could move his arms an inch or two, a circumstance of which he immediately took advantage to enlarge the small space round his head.

An attempt to move his feet, however, quickly proved to him that there was no possibility of wriggling himself out backward, for both legs were pinned down immovably. No; his one and only chance lay in going forward, if he could, and that chance, he recognized, was a very slender one.

However, his courage having returned, he determined not to yield without a struggle; and he immediately commenced operations by digging out handfuls of earth from the wall in front of him, and endeavouring to push the refuse past his body, behind. This he found to be possible, after a fashion, although he fully realized that the small empty spaces about him available for the purpose would soon be filled up. Still, if he could but manage to break down sufficient of the barrier cutting off his escape, his shouts, if loud enough, might possibly reach his friends, who would of course come at once to his rescue.

To this end he worked frenziedly, gaining a little more space by exerting all his strength and pushing upward, thus compressing the soft earth and giving him an appreciably larger area in which to move.

But he quickly realized that unless he could obtain speedy deliverance he must be suffocated. He accordingly lifted up his voice and shouted at the full pitch of his lungs; but from the dull muffled manner in which the sound rang in his ears he knew that his cries must be quite inaudible in the house, and he soon relinquished an effort which merely exhausted him without doing the least good.

Then, at the moment when he was on the point of despair, he remembered the musket he had captured from the sepoy. It had a long barrel, and with it he ought to be able to push a hole through the earth in front of him which would at least let in a little air and through which he might be able to communicate with the others. Also, he recollected in that instant that the piece was loaded, and hope again sprang up in his bosom.

Feeling for the muzzle, he lightly stuffed his pocket-handkerchief into the barrel, to prevent it becoming choked with earth and thus bursting when fired, and commenced to push it gently through the wall of earth.

This was no easy matter, and Chaloner was beginning to fear that he was cut off by a thicker barrier than he had imagined, when suddenly the resistance ceased, and the piece disappeared, right up to the trigger-guard. The muzzle, then, must be protruding into the pit in the back room, below the floor-boards!

Carefully wiping the soil from the hammer and from round the percussion-cap, Chaloner pulled the trigger, half expecting the breech to burst in his face.

There followed an explosion that sounded, in the confined space, like that of a powder-magazine, and the piece, recoiling, struck him a fearful blow on the cheek with the butt, laying it open as though with a knife. It also caused another slight shower of earth.

The seconds passed without result, and Chaloner nearly fainted as the idea occurred to him that perhaps Fairbanks and Shere Singh were not in the house at all!

Then he thought he heard a slight sound in front of him, and he immediately began to push the musket to and fro, so that the motion of the barrel might be observed. A moment later he felt the muzzle clutched and held, and he at once twisted it violently, to show that there was human motive power at the butt end.

The murmur of voices sounded a little plainer now, and he summoned all his strength for one great shout of: "Help, boys, help quickly, I am suffocating!"

Next moment the buzz of conversation sounded still more loudly, and he heard, as though from a vast distance, the reply: "Is that you, Peter?"

"Yes," shrieked Chaloner despairingly. "Hurry, Fairbanks, for Heaven's sake! I can't last much longer!"

Almost with his last word he felt the earth quiver a little as one of the rescuers dug savagely into it with a spade, and Shere Singh's voice was heard, like a whisper, bidding him bear up, as help was coming.

But by this time the unhappy lad's senses were fast leaving him; his eyes felt as though they were bursting from his head, his lungs felt on fire. Stars seemed to fill and dazzle the darkness, flashes of orange, scarlet, and purple seemed to sear his very brain, and his tongue felt too large for his mouth to contain it. He could no longer whisper, much less speak or shout, and the dead weight on his body was fast becoming intolerable. A thousand queer fancies whirled through his brain; he felt that his head and his lungs were bursting, and finally his agony became insupportable, his senses left him, and he knew no more.

. . . .

"A drop more of that brandy, Subâhdar Sahib; I think he swallowed those last few drops. And give me that pail of water, will you? I'll just dash another cup or so over his face. I'll swear that I can feel his heart beating now, and I believe we shall save the dear chap after all."

The voice, thought Chaloner dreamily to himself, as he slowly struggled back to consciousness, sounded very much like that of his old chum Fairbanks. And the deep, resonant voice that next sounded in his ears seemed remarkably like that of the Subâhdar. Shere Shingh seemed to be saying:

"Here you are, *Huzoor*; here is the brandy. Give

him a little more. I think the colour is coming back into his cheeks. And see—see, he breathes!"

At this Chaloner slowly opened his eyes, memory returned, the memory of that hideous experience of his in the tunnel, and he realized that he had escaped a frightful death by a very, very narrow margin. Shere Singh and Fairbanks were leaning over him as he lay on his narrow *charpoy* (camp bedstead), anxiety written all over their brown faces, one of them with a spirit bottle in his hand, and the other holding a tin cup of water into which he was just dipping his fingers. The sun was streaming brightly into the room through a kind of skylight in the roof, from which circumstance he gathered that they had carried him upstairs, unconscious, to his own bedroom.

"Allah be praised!" ejaculated Shere Singh. "Thou hast recovered then, *Huzoor*. Tell thy servant whether all is well with thee, for of a verity I believed thee dead when we pulled thee from that accursed hole nearly an hour agone."

"How do you feel, Peter, old chap?" was Fairbanks's contribution, delivered very heartily.

"Oh, all right!" returned Chaloner, moving slightly; "no bones or anything broken, I think; but I feel frightfully shaky."

"Shaky!" repeated Fairbanks. "By Jove! I should think so, after such an experience as yours. How did it happen, old chap?"

Chaloner struggled into a sitting posture, and after a good deal of coughing, to expel the dust from his lungs, gave his expectant audience a detailed account of his experiences from the time when he left the house some hours previously. When he had finished, Fairbanks and the dignified native officer expressed, in their separate manners, their joy at the near prospect of the intended storming of the city.

"We shall have to get after our information in grim earnest now," volunteered Fairbanks presently; "for our men will need all the help we can give them. But you must rest all day to-day, my friend, and we will remain to look after you; then, if you are well enough, we can all sally forth to-night, separately, and pick up what information we can."

So shaken was Chaloner by his recent experience that he could not but agree as to the wisdom of this proposal, which was accordingly carried out.

Before attempting anything else, however, it was necessary to clear the tunnel of the fallen earth, and in this task the whole day was spent by Fairbanks and the Subâhdar, working alternately, the tunnel being at the same time slightly enlarged and the earth pounded as hard as possible, so as to reduce the danger of the roof again falling in. The cause of the caving-in was believed to have been a British shell striking and exploding somewhere close at hand.

Darkness having at last fallen, and Chaloner by that time feeling practically himself again, the three companions cautiously left their house, and, separating, made their several ways into the town.

By arrangement Chaloner took the Chândni Chauk for his beat, after strolling up and down which street for an hour or so, without learning anything of interest, he turned into a brilliantly lit wine-garden, and took a seat well away from the crowd, at the same time calling for something to drink, so that he might appear to have a legitimate excuse for being there.

While slowly sipping his beverage he kept his eyes and ears open for the slightest hint of anything interesting in progress. But, so far as he could tell, every individual present seemed to be there merely to enjoy the passing hour, not to discuss matters of importance, such as the siege; and after sitting unprofitably for nearly an hour, he was about to give up his quest and return home for a good long night's sleep, which he sorely needed, when something suddenly occurred which caused him to alter his mind.

As has been mentioned, he was sitting well away from the crowd, where he could keep an eye on everything that happened, and was not aware that the thick hedge of flowering shrubs against which his seat was placed was not the boundary of the premises.

That it was not so was made plain by his suddenly hearing the sound of voices approaching behind him, mingled with the clink of cavalry spurs, and the occasional clash of a swinging scabbard.

A quick, furtive glance through the parted shrubs revealed the fact that another small, and possibly private, garden lay just beyond the hedge, and that across the lawn two *sowârs* were slowly striding, straight toward a stone seat which was placed just behind Chaloner's own, on the other side of the hedge.

The men were conversing very earnestly, with many excited gestures, and Chaloner decided that he would remain where he was, since they were undoubtedly discussing something of importance. Moreover, one of the two officers was Fuzl Aziz, while a remark made by the latter told the listener that Aziz's companion was none other than that redoubtable sepoy general, Mehtab Singh!

The next moment Chaloner allowed the shrubbery of the hedge to fall gradually and noiselessly back into place, and the two officers, utterly unsuspecting, flung themselves upon the stone seat.

For a few minutes the pair continued the discussion of a matter that had no interest for Chaloner. Then suddenly Mehtab Singh turned to his companion and said: "And now, tell me, what is this new plan of thine that thou desirest to discuss with me?"

CHAPTER XII

Plot and Counterplot

CHALONER edged a little farther along, and leaned back among the shrubs as far as possible, until only a couple of feet or so separated him from the schemers on the other side.

He also managed quietly to make a little spy-hole for himself through the hedge; for, although he remembered Fuzl Aziz's appearance well enough, he had, so far as he was aware, never set eyes on the notorious sepoy general, and he wanted to be able to recognize him again when he saw him.

The light from the numerous lanterns scattered about the garden and suspended from the branches of the trees showed him a man of considerable stature, perhaps a little over six feet, dressed in the regulation French-grey uniform and high black riding-boots. But that uniform was now embellished with numberless arabesques of gold lace, gold aiguillettes depended from the left shoulder and hung down over the man's breast, upon which glittered a few medals and an order or two, and the cuffs of his tunic sleeves were stiff with gold bullion. He wore epaulettes of gold lace, and his white turban was decorated with a single magnificent plume, fastened with a diamond clasp.

For the rest, Mehtab Singh was rather a handsome man, with a very dark complexion, heavy black moustache, twisted upward at the ends, and a beard, slightly tinged with grey, parted in the middle and brushed fiercely upward and outward on each side.

His eyes were deeply sunken, and shaded by heavy lids which gave him a perpetually drowsy expression, although he was really nothing of the kind, being a very energetic man; while the thin, tightly-compressed lips, barely showing between moustache and beard, gave certain evidence that his reputation for cruelty and severity had not been unjustly earned.

"It is this, General," began Fuzl Aziz. "You have doubtless observed that the *Farângi sûrs* have planted a breaching battery, which I believe they call Number Three, on the south side of the Kudsia Gardens, right alongside the old Custom House, and only two or three hundred feet from the Water Bastion. Now, that battery and Number Four Mortar Battery and Number Two Breaching Battery have been playing on that portion of the walls which lies between the Water Bastion and the Kashmir Bastion, with the result that a breach has been very nearly made at the north-east end of that length; and also—a very serious matter—so much damage has been done at the south-west end that a very little further battering at that point will bring the walls about our ears. Fortunately, the sons of *Sheitân* are not aware of the extent of the damage, or they would complete their work and come in through the breach—we could not prevent them!"

"Well," muttered Chaloner to himself, "that's interesting, at any rate. If the 'sons of *Sheitân*' don't yet know the fact, they shall to-night, or my name's not what it is. Thanks for your information, Fuzl Aziz! Pray continue."

As though in response to the Englishman's unspoken request, the sepoy officer at once continued.

"Now, General, our guns are so placed that we can keep down and hamper the fire from Number Two and

Number Four, but, try as we may, we cannot bring a single gun to bear on Number Three, the battery that is doing the most damage, and my men are not good enough riflemen to keep its fire down by musketry alone. But that battery must be destroyed, or we shall have the *Farângis* in on top of us before we know where we are. And my plan is this.

"I shall place a large party of sappers and miners at work, commencing close to the Water Bastion, and shall drive a mine under the walls, running the mine due north until its end reaches a point directly below that accursed battery. Then, when all is in readiness, I shall place several barrels of powder there, and blow battery and men to Gehenna. The ground at that point will then be so broken up that it will be impossible for the *Farângis* to plant any more guns, and we shall be safe from that quarter. What thinkest thou of my plan, General?"

There was silence for a few seconds, during which Chaloner strained every nerve to catch the first word; for English lives were hanging in the balance. Then Mehtab Singh delivered himself.

"It seems a good plan, Fuzl Aziz," he admitted thoughtfully, "and ought to succeed, provided the *Farângis* do not complete their work and get in before we can have the mine finished. How long, think you, will it take to run?"

"Not long," replied Aziz in a relieved tone; "since thy servant, believing that thy wisdom would approve the plan, commenced the work some days ago, and—the mine is almost ready to fire."

Chaloner started violently and nearly betrayed himself. The danger was much more imminent than he had imagined.

"Almost ready, sayest thou?" repeated the General. "That is good, my friend; thy zeal is indeed praiseworthy. When, exactly, dost thou think it will be ready?"

Fuzl Aziz deliberated for a few seconds, and then answered:

"I had hoped to be ready by noon to-morrow, but I fear that it cannot be done. By darkness to-morrow, though, everything will be complete, and we can fire the powder as soon as we like."

"Good!" ejaculated Mehtab Singh. "Now, listen to me, thou schemer. Do not blow up the battery to-morrow, for the gunners cease firing after dark, and we should only be able to destroy the guns. Wait until the next morning, when artillerymen and officers are at their posts, and *then* act! Thus wilt thou destroy perhaps a hundred men, as well as the guns; and the more *Farângis* we slay the better for us, for they have none too many men to spare."

"Thou shalt be obeyed, General," almost shouted Fuzl Aziz, slapping his thigh. "By Buddha! that plan likes me well. Kill! Kill! Kill the *Farângis*! Death to the pigs! Then, at noon of the day after to-morrow I myself will fire the mine; and thou, General, shalt stand on the walls and see the British blown to death!"

"Hush! hush, thou fool!" hissed Mehtab Singh. "Dost need to let all the city know thy plans? Thou canst never tell where spies may be lurking; and if this news gets noised about—well, I shall know whom to blame, that's all!"

"I crave thy pardon," said Fuzl Aziz in much more subdued tones; "but we know that here at least there can be none to overhear us. This is the private portion of the gardens."

"Maybe so," growled the other; "but didst ever know a spy heed what was or was not private? Look thou through this hedge behind us and thou wilt see that folk are nearer than thou thinkest. Near enough, at any rate, to hear thy shouting. I trust thou hast done no harm, Fuzl Aziz."

Chaloner started violently. If either of the men looked through or over the hedge they could not possibly avoid seeing him, and all would be lost. He must get away from this dangerous corner at once.

"Nobody could possibly have heard me, General," answered Fuzl Aziz somewhat surlily. "There are no tables or seats within twenty *guj* of the hedge. But, to prove that I speak truth, look for——"

The moment Mehtab Singh commanded Aziz to ascertain whether there was anybody in the vicinity, Chaloner had risen softly to his feet, and, keeping well in the shadow of the hedge, had started to walk rapidly away; and as he went he heard Fuzl Aziz's last remark. He also heard the sudden pause after the last word, and instantly knew that Aziz was watching him, as he strove to walk away unconcernedly.

He was then fully thirty feet away from the seat, but he knew that the mere presence of anyone so close to the hedge could not but strike the two officers as highly suspicious, and every second he expected to hear Aziz's voice calling upon him to stop.

By this time, however, he was approaching the entrance to the gardens, and a few more yards would put him outside the premises. Still no cry was raised behind him, although he felt that both Sepoys were watching, and he was beginning to think he would get safely away after all, when the proprietor of the place happened to catch sight of him, and came running toward him to be paid.

The man himself had no suspicion that Chaloner was being watched, but he did not wish to lose his money; so he called to the young man to stop. And, as though the shout had loosened the spring of Aziz's tongue, he too suddenly called out, in Ûrdu: "Hi, Ali, hi! stop that man there! Stop him, I say, thou dolt; seize him! Ah! fool that thou art, thou hast let him go! After him, all of ye; after him and catch him, though he run to Kashmir, *for he is a Farângi spy*!"

Chaloner was just thrusting his hand into his pocket for a coin with which to pay the landlord, when Aziz's voice rang loud and sharp through the silence, and it became clear to the young man that if he wanted to save his skin it was high time to be off.

The man Ali, after the first start of astonishment, flung out his hands and grasped the linen waistbelt of Chaloner's white robe; but, turning like lightning, Chaloner seized the fellow's wrists and, exerting all his strength, tore them free and ran like a deer for the exit, the whole garden ringing behind him with cries of rage and alarm; for most of the men there did not know what was happening.

Luckily, nobody was between him and the gate; but a quick glance rearward showed him a perfect arsenal of knives and swords flickering in the lantern light, and he knew that he was again going to experience the sensations of a hunted man.

By a stroke of great good fortune there was a road, very little used, exactly opposite the garden entrance: narrow, ill-paved, and scarcely illuminated at all, running at right angles to the street in which the wine-garden was situated; and into this Chaloner plunged—the whole pack in full cry at his heels—praying that he might not encounter anybody bold enough to try to stop him. He knew that in the main street he would have been stopped and borne down by superior numbers before he could have traversed a hundred yards, but in this unfrequented street he still had a fighting chance. So, setting his teeth, he darted along still more swiftly, drawing his sword from under his cloak as he ran, and then unbuckling and flinging away the empty scabbard, while behind him rang out sharply the clatter of military boots, the swift pad-padding of sandal-shod feet, and furious shouts of "*Dîn! dîn!* Slay the infidel! Stop him! Seize the spy!"

He knew that if he were finally to escape he must somehow throw his hunters off the scent, so he began to search his mind for some dodge by which he could evade the pursuers and make his way home at leisure afterwards.

Fortunately for him, the street he was in was a long one, not cut by many cross streets; so, having by this time got his second wind, Chaloner proceeded to force the pace, and soon had the satisfaction of hearing the chase dropping away behind.

Then suddenly, as he plunged into the black shadow cast by a great baobab-tree, he became aware that a house which he was passing was empty, and, swerving as he ran, he turned in at the open gate, and in another moment was effectually hidden among the shrubs. As he crouched there, recovering his breath, he presently heard his pursuers dash past. Then, allowing time for the last laggards also to pass, he calmly walked out of the garden again, retraced his steps a few yards until he came to a cross street, turned into this, and so, by a roundabout route, made his way back to the house under the ramparts, which, contrary to his expectation, he reached without encountering the slightest sign of his pursuers.

He knocked the signal agreed upon, and a moment later found himself in the dimly-lighted back room, where Fairbanks and Shere Singh were awaiting him in a state of the greatest anxiety, for he had never before been so late.

"Where on earth have you been, Peter?" asked his chum.

"Don't question me now," was the hurried reply,

"but get me something to eat and drink—quick! The safety of the whole breaching battery depends upon my reaching the camp to-night!"

The sight of Chaloner, haggard, dishevelled, breathless, and obviously labouring under the most intense excitement, added to his gasping ejaculation, apprised Fairbanks and the Subâhdar that something of vital import had occurred; and, like sensible people, they at once proceeded to minister to him without asking further inopportune questions. Shere Singh routed out brandy and food, while Fairbanks rushed upstairs to procure dry garments to replace those, streaming with perspiration, which now clung to his chum's limbs. A generous nip of spirit, a brisk towelling, a change of clothes, and a good meal acted upon Chaloner like magic; and presently, having recovered his breath, he related in detail to his companions the full particulars of his recent adventure, upon hearing which they fully agreed with him as to the imperative necessity for him to make his way to the British camp and impart his information to General Nicholson without a moment's unnecessary delay. Therefore, having finished his meal, the lieutenant rose and, accompanied by his two friends, made his way to the mouth of the tunnel, where, bidding his companions adieu, he plunged into the hole, and a few minutes later found himself outside the walls.

The night was intensely dark, the moon not having yet risen, while the stars were almost completely obscured by heavy clouds; but, having already passed over the ground, Chaloner now knew his way pretty well, and within an hour he reached the camp safely, and, after narrowly escaping being shot by the first sentry he encountered, was conducted to General Nicholson's tent. As he approached, it became evident that, late as was the hour, the general was still astir, for the tent was illuminated, and as the sentry outside halted him, and demanded his business, Chaloner caught the low murmur of voices in earnest conversation. A moment later, the sentry having announced him, he entered, to find Nicholson and several other officers seated round a camp-table.

"Good evening, Mr. Chaloner!" exclaimed Nicholson cordially. "Have you any more information for us? Yes, I see that you have. What is it this time? Anything important, eh? Take a seat and make yourself comfortable."

"Thank you, sir!" replied Chaloner, obeying. "Yes, it is rather serious, I am sorry to say." And he proceeded to explain in detail the events of the evening, ending up with his flight for life from Fuzl Aziz, Mehtab Singh, and the rest.

When he had finished, Nicholson remained for some little time sunk in deep thought, caressing his great, bushy black beard, as was his custom when worried about anything. Presently he said to Chaloner: "The mine with which these precious rascals intend to blow up the battery is to be fired, you say, at noon the day after to-morrow—or to-morrow, rather, since it is already some time past midnight?"

"That was the arrangement I overheard, sir," answered the young man. "But in my opinion, since they must very strongly suspect that their plot is known, they will not keep to their original arrangement, but will work with might and main to complete the job before then. I should say that Number Four will hardly be safe much after noon to-day."

Nicholson nodded vigorously. "That is my own idea," he said. "Only I think you have perhaps rather underestimated the time. I fancy the battery will be quite safe until, say, three or four o'clock in the afternoon. I have several reasons for thinking so. Now,

Baird-Smith," he went on, turning to the engineer officer sitting opposite him, "this is where you come in. There is about twelve hours' very hard work in front of you and your men. I am going to try to teach these sepoys a lesson, and this is the way I propose to do it. You will at once call a muster of the sappers and miners, get down to Number Four, and commence making a countermine beneath the battery, sinking it deep enough to allow the sepoy mine to run unhindered between our workings and the battery. By starting work at once, you ought, before daylight, to be out of eyeshot from the ramparts, safely hidden below ground. Of course you will only undermine the extremity of the mutineers' tunnel, for that is the spot where they will plant their own explosives; and, as soon as we hear the rascals—as we shall—getting ready to explode it, we will have the guns run back, fire off the countermine, and blow the sepoy tunnel—together with a goodly number of sepoys, I trust—to perdition. That should make them a little shy of trying on anything of the kind in future, and the debris of the explosion will form a splendid embankment behind which we can again run up the guns. What do you think of the plan, gentlemen? Can you manage to carry out your part in the time available, Baird-Smith?"

"To punish the mutineers so severely," answered the engineer, "my men and I would tackle a task twice as difficult—and complete it, sir. You may rely on us."

And he departed to rouse out his tired sappers and miners, in the midst of a subdued burst of applause, while several other officers filed out, determined to work with their own hands to help forward the work which Baird-Smith had undertaken to carry out.

Nicholson's big black eyes sparkled approval as he watched the men depart, and Chaloner wished heartily that he might have formed one of that noble band of officers who had sworn to capture Delhi or die in the attempt. But he had other and equally important work to do; therefore, receiving his dismissal, he saluted and retired, and five minutes later had left the British outposts behind and was picking his perilous way through the darkness toward the city walls, which he reached, half an hour later, without being observed, then plunged into the tunnel, to find Fairbanks and Shere Singh anxiously awaiting him at the other end.

At the hour arranged for the springing of the countermine Chaloner and his companions made their way to the battlements and looked anxiously in the direction of the threatened British battery.

Then the lieutenant uttered a suppressed cry, for it seemed to him that something must have gone wrong with Nicholson's arrangements. The battery was in its usual position, the gunners, as usual, loading and firing their pieces at certain sections of the walls as coolly and methodically as though there were no threatening mine within a thousand miles. Besides, he could not see a single trace of any of the countermining operations which Baird-Smith had undertaken to carry out. Everything wore its accustomed appearance, and, with a sinking of the heart, the young Englishman was compelled to believe that either a great error in the time available had been made, or else——

Suddenly, as he gazed, he saw a number of men on horseback appear like magic from behind a *topi* of trees, where they had been concealed, and gallop like fiends toward the guns.

A second glance showed that they were artillerymen, and that the horses had all their harness on their backs, the riders holding the loose traces and straps in one hand while they flogged with the other. At the same moment the gunners discharged their last round, sponged out their pieces, flung down sponges and rammers, and stood ready to connect up the limbers to the pieces as soon as the horses were attached.

A loud shout, audible even to the trio, a quick turn amid a whirlwind of dust, and when the dust slowly cleared away, the guns were already being drawn back from the entrenchment, the speed increasing every moment.

Then a bugle shrilled through the hot air, and on the instant a swarm of men carrying picks and shovels appeared to spring out of the solid earth, so cunningly had Baird-Smith concealed the situation of the entrance to his countermine.

These men ran, bending almost double in their eagerness to cover as much ground as possible in the shortest space of time; but one man, an officer, still lingered by the pit, careless of the sepoy bullets that flew round him like hail. In his hand he held something from which a slight spiral of smoke curled up into the palpitating air, and Chaloner at once recognized the calm, collected officer. It was Baird-Smith himself.

Meanwhile, although everything had happened with startling suddenness, the sepoys on the Water Bastion had by now realized that there was something in the wind, and there was a vast amount of shouting going on among them.

There was running up and down, waving of arms, and, worse than all, the panic of the sentinels was communicating itself to the dense throng below. Shrieks of agony began to rise shrilly above the shouting, as men, women, and children were crushed by those trying to push their way out, and a second or two later a body of passing cavalrymen, becoming alarmed, began to charge their horses through the press, stricken by the prevailing terror, for which they all, at the moment, were unable to account.

The heavy, curved cavalry swords began to rise and

fall in the morning sun, as the *sowârs* found their escape barred, and a wail of misery and despair arose from the unhappy beings who were themselves unable to move hand or foot because of the press.

Chaloner's gorge rose at the fearful sight and the still more dreadful sounds, and he turned his eyes once more in the direction of the battery.

As he did so he saw Baird-Smith suddenly stoop and place the smoking linstock to something which was undistinguishable at that distance but which he shrewdly suspected to be a train of powder.

Then the Engineer took to his heels and ran like a hare after his men, who were now quite a safe distance away.

There was a brief pause, during which a little puff of smoke filtered into the air, and then, as though by magic, the surface of the ground all round and about the site of the battery rose heavily upward for several yards, in what looked like a solid piece, immediately followed by a frightful burst of flame and smoke, as though a volcano had suddenly broken out. A moment later there came the shock of the explosion of over a ton of gunpowder, driving the air before it like a hurricane, and the ears of the watchers were assailed with a dull, heavy, deafening boom.

The sight was appalling, terrific, like nothing any of the trio had ever before seen or dreamed of; but there was worse to follow. For, as the tortured earth subsided once more, and fell into the pit formed by both the mine and the countermine, it naturally forced the white-hot fumes of the explosion back along the sepoy tunnel.

From the city end, round which the crowd was still gathered, unable to move, there came a perfect hell-blast of flame, which enveloped hundreds in its fiery embrace, and in a moment the garments of the people were torn from them, whirled aloft in sheets of flame, while the very flesh was scorched from their bones almost in the twinkling of an eye. The horrible sound of horses screaming in their death-agony mingled with the wailing cry of a dense mass of human beings suddenly faced by a frightful death from which there was no escape, a sound which, once heard, can never be forgotten.

Even the glass in the windows of the houses opposite was melted by that fiery blast, and already tongues of flame were beginning to flicker hideously here, there, and everywhere; and it quickly became evident to the three friends that they were witnessing a holocaust.

They could not help; they simply dared not try; therefore they did the next best thing—turned their backs upon the scene and hastened home.

As they reached their house, unable to converse or speak from sheer horror of the thing, they heard the dull booming of artillery commencing once more from the direction of the Water Bastion.

Nicholson, the indefatigable, the relentless, had again planted his guns on the wreck of the battery, and was even now re-commencing the shelling of the doomed city.

CHAPTER XIII

Captured

NEARLY a month had elapsed since that dreadful morning when Chaloner and his two friends had witnessed the catastrophe resulting from the blowing up of the sepoy mine, a month during which none of them had dared to venture out during daylight.

For, after the terror and excitement resulting from the destruction of two or three hundred people had somewhat subsided, the Powers in Delhi had naturally begun to ask themselves to what the failure of their carefully-matured plot had been due, and the answer was not far to seek. It simply resolved itself into the fact that someone must have obtained knowledge of the plans of the defenders, and have carried the news to the English camp.

Of course Fuzl Aziz and Mehtab Singh had no doubt as to the identity of the informant, for they had suspected all along that the man whom they had caught sight of in the wine-garden, and whom they had subsequently chased, had overheard their conversation, and that he was a spy in the service of the British. The result was such a strenuous hunt for the spies that in spite of all their precautions they had many narrow escapes, each escape of course being narrower than the last, and at length it became impossible for them to venture forth without instantly finding themselves the objects of marked suspicion. By the exercise of vast ingenuity they managed to appear in a different disguise almost every time they went out; yet people were gradually becoming accustomed to their general appearance, and, as nearly every man in the city was on the look-out for them, it began to appear as though the time were fast approaching when capture could not possibly be avoided any longer, and the three were beginning to find the strain becoming unendurable.

It was therefore with unfeigned thankfulness that, one night on his arrival at the camp, Chaloner was informed by Nicholson that the difficulties which had from time to time unexpectedly cropped up were now all overcome, and that their period of employment as secret agents in Delhi was therefore fast coming to a close.

Owing to the stringent watch that was being kept for them, they had not been able to collect nearly so much information as had been possible before the explosion, being only able to work at very infrequent intervals; consequently the period of a fortnight which Nicholson had originally mentioned as being the time when he expected to be able to deliver the final grand assault had lengthened into a month. But at last, the young Englishman was informed, preparations were all but complete, and it was confidently expected that in a couple of days Delhi would be once more in the hands of its legitimate possessors.

Nicholson's plans and arrangements had worked out as they always did, and every single man, officer and private, knew just what was going to happen, and what his share of the work was going to be. The little army, increased now to about five thousand men, all told (five thousand against one hundred and fifty thousand!), worked like a well-oiled machine, and there had been no hitch anywhere.

From his own observation Chaloner knew that the breaches made in the walls of Delhi by the great siege-cannon were now practicable for a strong, determined storming-party, particularly those near the Water Bastion and the Kashmir Gate; and he was able to give Nicholson and his officers a great deal of information about the means which the mutineers were adopting to defend those weak spots.

That the storming would be a very difficult matter, demanding an enormous amount of stubborn persistence, and inevitably involving a tremendous sacrifice of life, nobody could doubt; for, notwithstanding their innumerable faults, the mutineers were for the most part brave men, their officers were skilful, and all branches of the native army had been so thoroughly trained by the British themselves that it almost seemed as though the white men were fighting against their own troops. Added to all this, there was the fact that the defenders of the city outnumbered the beseigers by about thirty to one, and that the British would have to contend against that most murderous description of warfare, namely, street and house-to-house fighting, before an advance could be made into the heart of the city itself.

It was this portion of the forthcoming attack that was giving the British most cause for anxiety, and Nicholson had already made up his mind that he must be prepared to sacrifice fully one-quarter of his force for the mere privilege of gaining a foothold in the outskirts of the city.

Once this had been accomplished, however, it was anticipated that the mutineers would lose heart, and that the remainder of the task would prove comparatively easy.

Chaloner, having supplied all the information he possessed, and having spent a considerable amount of time wandering about the camp, chatting with officers and men, was on the point of leaving camp to return to Delhi, when he received a summons to return to General Nicholson's tent. Considerably surprised, he hastened back to the tent, where he found the General alone.

"Mr. Chaloner," he said, "since you left me, an hour ago, reports have reached me which have enabled me to complete my plans, and it is well that you should know that the assault will be delivered the day after to-morrow, at daybreak, or very shortly after. I expect to carry the Kashmir and Kabul Gates with the first rush—I am staking my plans on being able to do so—so it will be as well for you to make your escape from the city with your friends, by way of your tunnel, as early as you can to-morrow night, bringing with you the latest information about the enemy's movements that you can obtain. Colonel Chamberlain will see you, and receive your report, for I shall then be engaged on other matters.

"Now I think I have said all that there is to say, except to thank and compliment you once again on the admirable way in which you have carried out a very difficult task. Goodbye, Mr. Chaloner! May God be with you!"

"Goodbye, sir; goodbye!" replied Chaloner, strangely moved by Nicholson's kindly appreciation. And he turned and strode quickly out of the tent, stopping at the entrance for one last look at the man he reverenced so highly. Then he allowed the tent-flap to fall, and found himself in darkness.

So accustomed had Chaloner become to passing to and fro at night between the city and the British camp, and so complete was his knowledge of the position of every outpost, aye, and even every sentinel of the enemy, that, dark as was the night, he made his way back with safety and but little difficulty to the mouth of the tunnel, and, passing through into the house, found his friends anxiously awaiting his return as usual.

Naturally, they were overjoyed to learn that the moment of their deliverance was so near at hand; for since they had become the objects of suspicion of almost every individual whom they encountered in the streets, not only had life in Delhi become dangerous in the extreme, but, what was more to the point, they felt that they were encountering that danger to no adequate purpose. The difficulty of obtaining information of any value had at length become so great as to amount, practically, to an impossibility.

Nevertheless, there was one duty which Chaloner felt it incumbent upon him to perform before he finally discarded the rôle of spy and with his companions retired from the city, to enter it again as a unit of a conquering army, and it was this.

On their first visit to the Collector's house he had observed, hanging upon the wall of one of the smaller rooms, a big map depicting the entire city of Delhi, drawn to a scale sufficiently large to show not only the defences and every street, but also even the most insignificant by-lane and alley; and although he had at the moment regarded it without interest, latterly the idea had come to him that that map would be of the utmost value to General Nicholson, particularly if the weakest points in the defences and certain other information were indicated thereon. From the moment when this idea had first occurred to him he had made frequent attempts to secure the map, but unsuccessfully, the house being found to be held under such strict surveillance that any attempt to enter it must inevitably have resulted in immediate capture.

Yet the more he thought about it the more convinced was he that the map would be of inestimable value to the British leader, and its possession by him the means of saving very many lives. Therefore, since it was impossible to venture forth during the day, he determined to devote the ensuing night—the last opportunity he would have—to a final effort to secure it. And of course, as soon as he announced his intention, his two companions declared their determination to accompany him, so that he might not be obliged to face the danger of the attempt single-handed. With this understanding, therefore, they partook of the best meal their fast-dwindling resources afforded, and then retired to their sleeping-chamber to rest and pass the hours of daylight.

At length, when the declining sun had sunk to within a hand's breadth of the horizon, painting the tender blue-green of the western sky with a thousand gorgeous hues of flaming gold and scarlet and purple, and bathing the domes and pinnacles of Delhi in rosy light, the trio arose and leisurely proceeded to discuss the last meal, as they hoped, of which they would partake in that sordid little house beneath the ramparts.

By the time that they had finished their meal and completed their preparations for flight from the city, night had fallen, the stars were out and the street-lamps lighted, and the moment had arrived for them to start upon their hazardous enterprise. They therefore stole softly to the door and, opening it, cautiously reconnoitred the street. It happened to be, for the moment, absolutely deserted.

The three friends stole silently away, keeping in the shadow of the houses as much as possible, and in less than half an hour found themselves standing safely on the lawn behind the Collector's house, carefully watching, from the shelter of a clump of bushes, for a few minutes, to make sure that none of the rebel soldiery had forestalled them and taken up their abode on the premises.

Convinced at length that the coast was clear, they ran swiftly up the rusty, dry grass to the veranda, from which a French window gave entrance to the ground floor. A few seconds' manipulation with the latch sufficed to open it, and they passed into the hot, stuffy drawing-room, about which a horrible odour still lingered.

With a shudder of repulsion they turned away quickly and left the room, feeling their way to the cellar door, so as to avoid striking a light where it might be seen, and stumbled down the steps into the pitchy darkness. Presently they laid hands on one of the lanterns which they had hidden away for use on some such occasion as the present, and lighted it.

The flickering yellow flame presently burned up brightly, and they looked eagerly round to see whether the place had been visited since they were last there; and, so far as they could see, it had not.

"Jove," exclaimed Chaloner, "I'd forgotten that our uniforms are still here! Come along, friends, let's get into them. Off with these miserable old rags! Thank goodness we have done with these things for ever—at least, I hope so. I detest this secret-agent business, and never want any more of it; it does not seem the right kind of job for a gentleman, whatever General Nicholson may think or say to the contrary. However, I suppose he's right in declaring that somebody has to carry out this kind of work. Here you are, Subâhdar Sahib, here's your kit," he went on briskly, cutting the string which bound the clothing up in a bundle, "and here's yours, Neville, my boy, and here's my own."

The change from the rags which they had been wearing into their own clothes was quickly effected, and then Chaloner turned to his companions.

"Gad," he exclaimed, "it is good to find oneself in uniform again, even though that uniform be considerably the worse for wear. Once more I feel—as I have not felt for a long time—that I am a British soldier. Are you fellows ready? Then up we go to the Collector's office and get that map; then hey for the British camp and decent companionship again! Put out that lantern, Subâhdar Sahib; we dare not take it upstairs with us, lest the light should be—— Hark! What is that?"

"That" was the unmistakable tramp of many feet and the clank of weapons immediately outside the house.

"Marked down, followed, and trapped at last!" exclaimed Chaloner bitterly. "There is no escape for us now, for of course they will make for this cellar the first thing. But, by heavens! they have not taken us yet. Out swords, and we will show the scoundrels how Britons can die. Here they are!"

There they were indeed.

As the three friends whipped out their swords, and stood on guard, resolved to sell their lives dearly, the house resounded with the heavy, eager tread of the man-hunters looking for their prey, the ring of steel, and the tumult of harsh, cruel voices; and the next second the cellar door flew open with a crash, revealing fully a dozen grey-coated *sowârs* at the head of the stairs, Fuzl Aziz and Chunder Lâl foremost amongst them.

All held drawn swords, these glittering ominously in the light of the flickering lantern on the cellar floor, which had not yet been extinguished; while the two leaders carried revolvers in addition to their swords, which they immediately levelled at the men whom they had at last trapped after so many months of fruitless endeavour.

"Surrender, ye infidel dogs," howled Fuzl Aziz in English, "surrender yourselves! Your hour has come at last, and there is no escape. There are twelve of us here, and the house is surrounded by a hundred more. Throw down your weapons and come up here!"

Chaloner fixed his eyes on the speaker and gave vent to a short, mocking laugh. "One hundred and twelve men are needed to take three—two of them lads," he jeered. "Truly art thou a brave man—also cautious, Fuzl Aziz, thou black-hearted slayer of women, thou betrayer of thy salt. You bid us come up to thee! Who art thou to give us orders? If thou dost want us, come and take us. Or, if thou art afraid, whistle up some more of thy dogs, and set them to the work thou fearest to do thyself."

At these words, uttered in the presence of his own men, words the biting contempt of which seemed to scorch his very brain, Fuzl Aziz became convulsed with fury. He tried to find words, but they choked in his throat, and he could only grind his teeth in a perfect frenzy of wrath.

Shere Singh himself laughed, and under his breath spoke to Chaloner. "Well done, *Huzoor*!" he whispered. "Thou art wise in what thou doest. Taunt the man but a little more and we shall be slain outright—we do not wish to endure the slow death he would prefer to give us. Continue to mock him until he shoots us down."

And indeed that is just what the raving Fuzl Aziz was about to do. He had already turned to order his men to fire a volley, when Chunder Lâl plucked him by the sleeve and whispered something in his ear.

The native officer listened, swallowed hard, and then gave another order, in Ûrdu, to his followers, at the same time stepping aside himself; and as he did so his men streamed down the cellar steps in a living wave and hurled themselves upon the three.

There was a short, fierce fight. In five minutes they

C 745

"'YE CROW NOT SO SHRILLY NOW, MY BANTAMS,' HE SNEERED"

were lying wounded and bound on the damp cellar floor, Shere Singh, poor fellow, with his arm slashed open from wrist to elbow, two bayonet wounds in his body, and his face laid open to the bone by a *tulwâr* slash; Fairbanks with a very nasty cut on the forehead that had all but stunned him; and Chaloner with a thrust through the thigh which had brought him to the ground.

When they had been thoroughly secured, and not till then, Fuzl Aziz came down the steps, stood over them, and commenced taunting them.

"Ye crow not so shrilly now, my bantams," he sneered. "Long have ye eluded and defied me, but the trap has snapped at last, and ye are in my power. How like ye the prospect? I shall have a few questions to ask ye later on, with regard to the *Farângis* outside, which ye will do well to answer—thou, I mean," kicking poor Chaloner violently in the ribs. "After that, if ye answer well and truly, I will grant ye all a merciful death. But if ye refuse, or play me false, then shall ye die a special death that shall be spoken of in India with horror for a hundred years. What say ye to that?"

"Nothing," replied the Englishman, "except this. You can make up your evil mind that do what you may you will not get me—or any of us, for that matter—to give you a single item of information respecting the British movements or their plans."

Fuzl Aziz, his teeth fairly chattering with rage and spite, raised his *tulwâr* preparatory to striking the helpless lad. Then, by an effort, he mastered himself, thrust the weapon back into its scabbard with a clash, spat viciously in Chaloner's direction, and, turning on his heel, shouted something in Ûrdu to the *Naïk* (corporal) in charge of the squad of *sowârs*, and rushed hastily up the cellar stairs, afraid to trust himself any longer within hearing of the Englishman's scathing tongue.

Immediately upon the native officer's command, the *Naïk* sent off half a dozen of the troopers, who returned in about ten minutes with three very roughly constructed litters, made from boughs of trees cut down in the garden, and upon these the three helpless prisoners were placed. Then, with four men to each, the litters and their burdens were picked up, carried up the stairs, through the house, and out into the street, the bearers immediately stepping out hurriedly, as though anxious to reach their destination before too many people became aware of the fact that they were performing the menial duty of carrying certain of the hated sahibs. Chunder Lâl and the *Naïk* walked at the head of the little procession, conversing eagerly together in low tones which they were apparently unwilling that the rest of the *sowârs* should overhear, while of Fuzl Aziz there was no sign. Having actually witnessed the capture of his enemies he had evidently gone on ahead to complete his arrangements with regard to the fate in store for them.

For the three prisoners the journey was a trying one. The men who carried them loaded them with insults, called them by the worst names their foul minds could think of, and invented among themselves all kinds of horrible tortures which they proposed Fuzl Aziz should try upon his victims. They also allowed the mongrel populace to approach the litters, to spit upon and strike the helpless men, even going so far as to encourage the few who seemed afraid of what the consequences might be if they were to strike one of the sahibs.

But if the ruffianly troopers fancied that the insults and ill-treatment heaped upon the prisoners were going to cause them to exhibit any symptoms of fear or indignation they were very much mistaken. The trio appeared to be absolutely insensible to the presence of anybody but their three selves, and they maintained a continuous conversation—in which they did not attempt to spare the feelings of their captors—the whole time they were being carried through the streets; and, by the time that their destination was reached, more than one of the *sowârs* would gladly have forfeited a year's pay for the privilege of executing the captives with his own hand.

At last, amid cries of excitement and execration, foul insults and blood-curdling threats, accompanied by showers of sticks, stones, clods of earth, and any other missiles that came handy, the little procession left the teeming streets, and, passing through the massive gates of iron and marble, entered the courtyard of the palace, where Fuzl Aziz, accompanied now by the mutineer general, Mehtab Singh, was impatiently awaiting their arrival.

Crossing the marble-flagged courtyard, the party passed through a small door set in the thickness of a high wall, and at once found themselves in the magnificent gardens at the rear of the building. The three captives were carried swiftly along the smooth, neatly gravelled footpaths, gleaming white in the light of the splendid tropic moon, past marble basins filled with brilliantly-hued fish—the pets of one of the numerous royal princesses—past magnificent fountains, the musical splashing of which sounded tantalizingly in the ears of the wounded prisoners, and through groves of beautiful trees and shrubs, until they came to a large marble building, adorned with mosaics in jade, malachite, and other valuable stones, which had the appearance of being one of the secondary palaces set aside for the accommodation of one or other of the three princes.

Fuzl Aziz rapped sharply on the door with the hilt of his sabre, and almost immediately it flew open, revealing an interior the luxury and magnificence of which Chaloner and Fairbanks had heard described, but of which the reality far surpassed even their wildest dreams. It was, as they quickly realized, the residence of that debauchee and demon in human form, Prince Abûl Bûkr, the drunkard, the man who had been more active than any of his fellow-ruffians in hunting down and slaying British fugitives, more particularly their womankind; the creature who, when later on shot so justly by Major Hodson's own hand, declared that he could die happy, as he had lived to see English women dragged through the streets of Delhi!

At last, after traversing what seemed to them to be an endless succession of corridors and passages, they came to the top of a flight of marble stairs. Down they were carried, Fuzl Aziz and Mehtab Singh still leading the way, and at last they reached a door beside which the two officers had halted.

"Carry them inside there," commanded Aziz sharply; "loose their ankles so that they can stand, but not their wrists; then draw your swords and stand guard over the prisoners while his Excellency and I question them. Thou, Dalil," he went on, speaking to the *Naïk*, "go and find the *Babu*, Iknam, His Highness's secretary, and tell him to come here bringing with him parchment and quills. I want him to take down the replies of these *Farângi* dogs as I put the queries."

Chaloner smiled. It was on the tip of his tongue to tell Fuzl Aziz that the man Iknam might as well save himself the trouble of coming, if that was what his services were needed for; but he decided not to be rash. Every minute's delay gained now was so much to the good, and if the evil hour could only be postponed long enough, there might, even now, be a slender chance for life. It was evident that neither Mehtab Singh nor Fuzl Aziz was at all conversant with the British plans—John Nicholson had a strangely keen nose for scenting out native spies—and that, therefore, they were entirely in the dark as to the projected attack which, all being well, was to take place at daybreak on the morrow, only about eight short hours thence.

In accordance with Fuzl Aziz's order, the prisoners had been carried, still on the litters, into a big apartment furnished only with a fine table, made of teak, and a few chairs, and the *sowârs* were now engaged in cutting the ropes which bound their ankles. Fuzl Aziz and the general had seated themselves at the table, Chunder Lâl was standing behind his master, looking down upon him with the curiously malignant expression which Chaloner had noticed upon a former occasion; and the *Babu*, who had now arrived in answer to the summons, was laying out his parchment, ink, and pens on the table preparatory to rolling up his wide sleeves and commencing work.

In the little pause that ensued, while Fuzl Aziz and Mehtab Singh carried on a short conversation in whispers, the three friends occupied themselves in trying to get the circulation back into their stiffened legs, and, while doing so, contrived to exchange just the few words that were necessary to enable them to tell the same story.

Then, suddenly, "Stand up, all of ye!" ordered Fuzl Aziz, drawing his chair up to the table, "and take heed that ye answer truly the questions I shall put to ye. Ye have not forgotten what I said in the cellar—ye will do well to choose the easy death.

"Now, you," he went on, addressing Chaloner; "you are the man who disclosed all our plans to Nikalseyn—do not deny it, for I know you did. You it was who enabled him to lay a mine that killed nearly three hundred of the Faithful—I know that too. Tell me, then, how did you go in and out of the city without our sentries discovering you? You could not have passed without the words, and those, I am ready to swear, you never learnt."

"Thou art right there," replied Chaloner. "I never knew a single password; but how I got in and out without it I leave to thy cleverness to discover. I refuse to say."

"Beware, beware!" growled Aziz, his eyes snapping vindictively. "You heard what I said."

"If the Infidel will not speak, I can tell thee," purred Chunder Lâl over his master's shoulder. "The house which they occupy has been perpetually watched by me. I saw them leave it to-night, and while I and some of my party tracked them to the Collector's house, others broke into and examined their abode, discovering a tunnel under the ramparts, through which the spies have undoubtedly been wont to pass at night between the city and the *Farângi* camp."

"Ha, is that so?" exclaimed Aziz. "Then I have learned something, in spite of thee, *Farângi*. Know any other of thy countrymen aught of this passage into the city?"

Chaloner considered a moment; an idea had just occurred to him. Then, "Yes," he answered; "there is no harm in telling thee that. They do know of it." And he smiled meaningly.

Aziz shifted uneasily in his chair. "Thou fool," he growled, glaring at Chunder Lâl, "why didst not inform me of this before? Thou, Dalil," turning to the *Naïk*, "hasten to the barracks; say I sent thee; and instruct the officer on duty to send a dozen men and a *Havildar* (sergeant) to the house. They are to fill in that passage at once, and block it so effectively that it may not again be passed.

"So," sneered Aziz, after the *Naïk* had left the chamber, "that is how thou hast managed to outwit us, *Farângi*? I wondered why it was that I never caught thee or those others in any of the nets I spread. But I have ye all now," he went on triumphantly, "and ye will carry no more secrets to your brethren.

Nikalseyn will have to do without his information henceforth—unless your ghosts have the power to talk to him. Now tell me, and tell truly, how goes it in the *Farângi* camp? How many men, how many guns, are outside there? How soon does Nikalseyn intend to murder his troops by flinging them against this city, which will never be captured by him?"

"All goes well in the British camp," Chaloner replied. "That I need not hesitate to tell thee. When Nicholson Sahib will send his men to take Delhi I would not tell thee even if I knew. But as for thy boast that he will never take it—thou must be mad as well as a fool if thou believest what thou sayest. Didst ever know Nicholson Sahib put his hand to aught and draw back? Didst ever hear of him breaking his spoken word? Thou knowest, as well as I, that if he has sworn to take Delhi, take it he will, though the heavens fall; and I can tell thee that he has so sworn. The numbers of men and of guns thou wilt learn for thyself all too soon for thy pleasure. Now I have spoken, and thou needst question me no more, for I have told thee all that I intend to tell. Make the most of it, Fuzl Aziz, betrayer of thy salt!"

"All that thou intendest to say, forsooth!" mocked Aziz. "All thou intendest to say, maybe; but not all that thou *wilt* say—be sure of that! When I bid a prisoner speak, that man obeys—sooner or later. Thou hast thy choice; what wilt thou do? Wilt answer here and now, without torture, or at the end of a few days—with it? Decide what thou wilt do, and that quickly, for I do not intend to waste time over any of ye; and I shall not ask again. Bear in mind this, also: thy refusal to speak will mean that thy two friends here will share thy torments as well. Thy silence sentences them, so think before thou speakest the words that shall not be withdrawn."

Fairbanks and Shere Singh were on the point of declaring forcibly that any threats levelled against themselves should not be allowed to deter Chaloner from his resolution to keep silence, when he managed to catch the eye of both of them and signalled them to say nothing.

Then, affecting to consider this new aspect of the case, after a few seconds apparently spent in deep thought, Chaloner remarked: "'Tis indeed what I should have expected of thee, thou hound, that thou shouldst be capable of torturing innocent men in order to gain thine own ends. I cannot decide what to do until I have spoken with my friends. I will not accept the responsibility without consulting them. Give us leave, therefore, to withdraw for a little time to some place where we shall not be overheard, and loosen, also, our wrists."

"No," thundered Aziz, "I will not give thee leave. Thou shalt decide for thyself. I wonder that I have bandied words with thee so long as I have. Speak now, and tell me thy decision."

At this moment Mehtab Singh whispered in Aziz's ear, and presently the latter nodded sulkily.

"His Excellency has spoken in thy favour," he growled, "and so thou shalt have thy wish. Ye may withdraw to the end of the room, yonder, where thou wilt not be overheard. But—no tricks, or it will be the worse for ye all!"

Accordingly the three went to the spot indicated, the *sowârs* and the two native officers, after cutting the ropes that bound their wrists, watching them like cats, ready to act at the first indication of an attempt to escape.

Poor Shere Singh, what with the pain from his torn arm and the two bayonet-wounds in his body, was all but delirious, and hardly capable of remaining on his feet, while Fairbanks and Chaloner were both suffering considerably from their own hurts; but it did not take any of them a second to decide that none of them would give up one word of information. Indeed, Fairbanks asked rather querulously why Chaloner had thought it necessary to prolong the ordeal by even a pretence of discussing the matter. It needed no discussion, he said.

"True," replied Chaloner in a low voice. "But we are in a very awkward fix, and have no hope whatever, that I can see. We can scarcely escape being tortured, but—I want to delay the evil moment as long as possible. Every minute that passes now brings the hour of the attack nearer. It is late already, and if we can only hold this demon off a few hours longer he will be far too busy with other matters to think of torturing us. Therefore I am doing this simply to waste time; and I shall fight for every possible moment of delay."

"I understand," whispered Fairbanks, "and will back you up all I can; and—— Look out, Peter! Catch him; he's falling," he suddenly interrupted himself, stretching out his arms; and, before Chaloner could turn round, Shere Singh, fainting from pain, lurched against them both, bringing them to the floor in his fall, which they managed to break slightly.

"Poor old chap!" exclaimed Chaloner. "Look here, Fairbanks, his tunic below the arm is simply soaking with blood; and—great Scot! his left riding-boot is full of it."

"By Allah!" broke in Fuzl Aziz's raucous voice, quivering with passion; "what is this, now? What is wrong with that Sikh dog? Does he think to avoid his punishment by pretending to be dead? Here, let me at him!" he shouted, roughly flinging the Englishman to one side; "I'll soon bring him to his senses!"

And he kicked the senseless man full in the face with his spurred boot.

"You infernal scoundrel," fairly howled Chaloner, rising to his feet stiffly, "you shall pay for that, if I die!" And, collecting his strength, he struck Aziz a terrific blow full on the point of the jaw, literally lifting the fellow off his feet and hurling him against the wall with a crash.

The man's head struck the hard marble with terrific force, and, with a strangled cry, he collapsed upon the ground and lay there senseless, the blood from his bitten tongue trickling out of the corner of his mouth on to the floor in a tiny crimson stream.

In a second the *sowârs* on guard leaped forward with cries of rage, their sabres pointed for a thrust, and the two lads thought that at last their hour had indeed come.

But before the men could carry out their intention the strident voice of Mehtab Singh made itself heard above the uproar.

"Drop your weapons!" he shouted. "Drop them, I say. Am I not your general? Very well, then," as the men sullenly lowered the points of their weapons, "see that ye obey my orders! That man yonder brought this on himself, and he deserves what he got. I am no friend to either *Farângi* or Sikh, but a man who will kick a senseless body—pah!

"Take him up, two of ye," he commanded to the troopers, "and carry him to his own apartments. The rest take up the body of the Sikh—he may still be alive—and convey him and these two *Farângis* to the room at the foot of the west turret. Lock them in there, and post a guard over the door."

Then, turning to Chaloner and Fairbanks, he added sternly: "Think not, because of this respite, that ye are to escape. In the morning, when Fuzl Aziz has recovered his senses, ye will be brought before us again; and if ye do not then reply, what has been promised ye, that shall be carried out, for it is necessary for me to know that which ye can tell if ye please. So consider the matter well this night, while ye have time. No further delay will be permitted after to-morrow morning."

Then, to the *sowârs*:

"Remove them, and keep them safe. Your own lives will answer for theirs, or for their escape."

Mehtab Singh then turned on his heel and quitted the room.

Two of the troopers picked up Fuzl Aziz—none too gently, for they had not forgotten the menial services to which he had put them—and, taking him one under the armpits and one by the legs, disappeared from the room and tramped off down the marble-flagged corridor with their burden. The other *sowârs*, some carrying Shere Singh, and the rest guarding their prisoners with drawn sabres, marched them off to the chamber indicated by Mehtab Singh, in a four-square, one-storied building, partially detached from the palace itself, and standing at the foot of one of the high domed turrets at the western extremity of the building.

The chamber itself was fairly comfortably furnished, as they discovered after they had been thrust inside and the door locked, and they had time to look round them.

It contained a divan, covered with silken cushions, upon which the senseless form of Shere Singh had been laid; there was a thick Persian carpet on the floor, a few short-legged, ebony coffee-tables stood about in various corners of the room, and there were plenty of quilted rugs and cushions upon which they could either sit or lie down.

In fact, the only visible evidence that the place could

be used as a prison consisted of the heavy teak-wood door, strongly reinforced with thick wrought-iron straps, which would easily stop even a rifle bullet; and the square window, without glass, but fitted with stout iron bars set in the thickness of the wall, at such close intervals that it would have been impossible for even the most slender of human beings to squeeze between them and escape.

The apartment evidently was one of those prisons, found in nearly every Eastern house of importance, in which the owner of the premises was accustomed to confine any members of his household who, in his opinion, required a little disciplining; and it was constructed so that anybody who might be imprisoned therein would undoubtedly remain there until it should please his jailer to release him.

The two lads wasted no more time on examining the chamber than was necessary to convince them that escape was utterly out of the question; then they immediately undertook the task of trying to revive the unconscious Subâhdar, who still lay as he had been placed, quite oblivious to his surroundings, but occasionally emitting a hollow, muffled groan of anguish which even his unconscious condition was powerless to deaden entirely. They had been thus engaged for about half an hour, unsuccessfully, and were still doing what they could to revive the old man, when Chaloner suddenly sprang to his feet.

"What the dickens was that?" he exclaimed.

"What was what?" asked Fairbanks, staring at his friend.

"Why," answered Chaloner, "something hit me on the back of the head, some small object. I felt it distinctly."

"Bit of plaster from the ceiling perhaps," suggested the other, gazing upward. "No, it couldn't have been that," he corrected himself, "because the ceiling, like the floor, is of marble. Ah!" he exclaimed suddenly; "how about the window? Perhaps it came through that?"

"Somebody trying to attract our attention from outside, eh?" exclaimed Chaloner. "Well, let's see."

He stepped softly across to the window, placed one of the low tables on the floor beside it, clambered up on it, and looked out.

The next second he turned excitedly to address Fairbanks.

"By Jove, Fairbanks, you're right!" he whispered. "There *is* somebody out there. A woman, apparently. And—*she looks to me like a white woman*!"

"Surely not," exclaimed Fairbanks excitedly. "It *can't* be! And yet—— By heavens! Peter, if it is so, I'll bet anything that that arch-scoundrel, Abûl Bûkr, the prince, is responsible for her being here, and that she is perhaps trying to effect her escape. Has she seen you? Here! here's a pebble—the one she threw in, maybe. Toss it out, and try to attract her attention."

"Hsh! hsh!" whispered his friend. "Stop talking, or the guard outside the door'll hear you. It's all right. She has seen me. She looks scared out of her life, poor soul, and—— Oh! good heavens! it's Miss Graham!"

"Nonsense, Peter!" retorted Fairbanks; "you're dreaming."

"I'm not," asserted Chaloner. "Come and look for yourself. Miss Graham! Miss Graham!" he whispered, as loudly as he dared. "We are Lieutenant Chaloner and Mr Fairbanks. You threw that pebble in to attract attention, didn't you? Did you know it was us——?"

"Not so loud, Mr. Chaloner," murmured the soft,

well-remembered voice from beneath the window. "There is no time to tell you everything, but matters did not turn out as we hoped. Mr. Williamson and I all but got away altogether, but we were captured within a few miles of safety. I was brought here a month ago—have been here ever since—and I do not know what happened to poor Mr. Williamson. I have not been actually badly treated, so far. To-night I heard that two Englishmen and one Sikh had been captured, and I at once guessed that—— Oh! heaven have mercy!" she shrieked suddenly, as foot-steps sounded on the gravel of the path, "I am discovered!"

The footsteps, vacillating in a peculiar manner, suddenly stopped, then came nearer again, quickly, while a thick, hoarse voice—the voice of a man far gone in liquor—roared out something in Ûrdu which none of them, fortunately perhaps, understood. There was a sudden scurry of gravel, then the sound of a heavy blow, and a woman's scream, quickly stifled, followed by a noise as of something heavy being dragged violently along the narrow path.

Chaloner at the window uttered a frightful imprecation, and shook the bars wildly. For a few seconds the lad foamed and raved like a madman; then he leapt to the floor, his face white as death, his eyes shining like live coals.

"The scoundrel! the—the *infernal, inhuman scoundrel*!" he choked. "Fairbanks, it was that demon, Abûl Bûkr. He came behind her, caught her by the shoulder, laughed in her face—the drunken brute—and struck her senseless. Then he dragged her away like a sack of coal. May heaven in justice let me live until I have driven my sword through that villain prince's heart, and I will die content. Oh!" he moaned, "to think that such things as these can happen under a man's eyes, and he be powerless to prevent them. Surely vengeance must be at hand!"

It was—close at hand.

CHAPTER XIV

To be Blown from the Guns

THEIR efforts to restore Shere Singh to consciousness were at last crowned with success, and the trio were chatting quietly together when they became aware that day was breaking; and while they were indulging in certain speculations as to what it had in store for them, the boom of a heavy gun broke in upon the silence of the early morning.

"Ha! did you hear that, Peter?" exclaimed Fairbanks excitedly. "The Great Day has dawned at last, unless I'm very much mistaken. That was a big gun!"

"It was," replied Chaloner, "and, what's more, there's another—and another—and another. Hurrah! the ball is opened, and I believe we shall wriggle out of this mess after all. But I am most dreadfully concerned on Miss Graham's account," he continued more soberly. "Goodness only knows what happened to her after that brute, Abûl Bûkr, struck her senseless and dragged her away. Besides, when once our troops have gained the city, she—and we too for that matter—will be in the greatest danger from the mutineers. In their rage and desperation you may be sure that they will try to butcher every European they may happen to hold captive, before the British can rescue them. That's the time when we shall have to look out for trouble. And, by Jove," he continued, "it's coming now!" as the sound of marching men was heard approaching along the corridor outside.

A second or two later there came the clash of grounded musket-butts, a key rattled in the lock, the door was flung violently open, and General Mehtab Singh entered, fully armed, a scowl of rage and hatred on his face, while a dozen sepoys with fixed bayonets streamed into the room behind him. There was tragedy in the air.

"Ye dogs," he hissed, the veins on his forehead swelling with anger, "this is your work, I know. 'Tis owing to your spying that the *Farângi* commander is attacking to-day—*at all our weakest points*. How should he have known, but for you, the very spots where we are most defenceless? By Shiv! I would that ye each had twenty lives, that I could wring each one of them from ye bit by bit! Had I but the time I would make ye pay in blood and tears for what ye have done—ye and others. But Delhi is not taken yet; the city still stands, and shall stand until I have prepared a proper welcome for your countrymen.

"Know, ye spawn of *Sheitan*," he continued, almost foaming at the mouth, "that inside the Kabul Gate, where Nikalseyn even now cheers on his men, there are guns—cannon—drawn up. These guns are loaded to the muzzle with grape and chain-shot, but we have no solid shot for them. Ye are going to serve instead, ye and that ancient hound yonder on the divan. Lashed to boards shall ye be, those boards in turn bound to the muzzles of the guns, and at the moment when the gates go down and your men come in, then shall the guns be fired, and the fragments of your bodies shall help to mow down your own friends." And he laughed, a hideous, high-pitched cachinnation that showed the two lads that he was now capable of any diabolical atrocity.

Suddenly the horrible laughter ceased, and Mehtab Singh struck his forehead with his clenched fist.

"Fool that I am," he shouted, "to waste time thus! Why, even at this moment they may have blown the gate in. Seize and bind those men," he snarled to the *havildar* in charge of the squad, "and bring them along —quick!"

The sepoys dashed in, and, before they had time to realize what was happening, Fairbanks and Chaloner found their hands pinioned—in front of them this time —while the Subâhdar, again unconscious, was snatched roughly from the divan and carried off by four men, the remainder at once hustling the two lads out of the door and into the palace grounds after him.

Mehtab Singh uttered a sharp word of command, and the little party swung off down the gravelled path, through the magnificent gardens, to a little gate in the wall, out of which they issued, finding themselves at once in the teeming streets of a city given over entirely to panic; the populace now being intent only on saving themselves, with as many of their belongings as they could carry away, from the swords of the avenging sahibs.

They could still find time, however, in passing, to jeer at the helpless captives being hurried away to a dreadful, humiliating death, and to fling stones at them, and try to snatch them fom the sepoys in order to tear them to pieces. And had it not been for the presence of Mehtab Singh it is very probable that they would have succeeded; for four men out of the dozen were fully occupied with carrying Shere Singh, while the others had to guard the prisoners and at the same time clear a path for themselves through the crowded streets.

Meanwhile the sun had been above the horizon for nearly an hour, and the white-hot glare of an Indian summer's day was already beginning to make itself felt.

The shimmering atmosphere vibrated to the thundering concussions of the heavy siege-cannon, and in the intervals could be heard the sharper, more ringing reports of the numerous field-pieces, which seemed to be directing their fire entirely on the western side of the city, somewhere between the Kashmir and Kabul Gates; thus making it plain that Nicholson was adhering to the plan of attack which he had outlined to Chaloner two evenings ago.

Now and again, too, as they approached closer to the ramparts, they could hear the regular *crash! crash! crash!* of volley-firing, mingled with rousing British cheers; and, staring death in the face though they were, they could not refrain from joining in the cheers themselves, to the utter amazement of the populace, and the almost maniacal indignation of their sepoy guard.

Time after time Mehtab Singh bade them keep silence, and threatened them with his sword, but they laughed in his face. Let the man slay them if he would; what did they care? A quick death by the sword would have been infinitely preferable to spending several hours in suspense, bound to the muzzle of a gun, knowing that there was practically no hope of escape, and that at the last their bodies would be blown to the winds by the same discharge that was intended to sweep others of their countrymen into eternity.

Finally, finding that it was impossible to intimidate the lads, the general gave up the attempt, and contented himself with swearing at his men for not making quicker progress through the crowd.

The party had by this time entered the zone of the British shell-fire, and shells came hurtling through the air above their heads, exploding with a horrible shattering crash against the walls or roofs of near-by houses.

It would be a most cruel stroke of fate if, after all, they were to be slain by their own friends, men who would have risked their lives to try to save them. Many a time during that last half-mile did the lads think that their hour had struck, for on several occasions shells dropped among the crowd quite close to them, sometimes failing to explode, and only killing one or two people by their impact alone, at other times exploding in the air and scattering fragments here, there, and everywhere, or else bursting upon striking the ground, in which case the execution done among the closely-packed masses was frightful.

A splinter from a shell filled with shrapnel, that burst fifty feet or more above the street, tore Chaloner's turban from his head, and then knocked out the brains of the sepoy marching beside him; but so far as he himself was actually concerned his skin was not even scratched, although he felt a bit dazed by the shock.

He commanded a sepoy to pick up the turban and place it on his head again, since his own hands were bound, never expecting to be obeyed; but, to his astonishment, the fellow did as he was told, overawed, apparently, by the self-possession of a man who could speak so calmly after such a narrow escape from death.

At last the crowd of inhabitants striving to get away began to get less dense, their places being taken more and more, as the ramparts were approached, by the actual defenders of Delhi, the sepoys and *sowârs*, who, to give them their due, were fighting like demons, prepared to hold the city to the last gasp, prepared to count their lives well lost if the hated *Farângi* could but be kept outside.

In their inmost hearts, however, they knew pretty certainly what the final result would be—the British must win at the last, even though, as Mehtab Singh had said, a warm reception had been prepared for them as soon as the gates had been stormed, particularly at the Kabul Gate, the conformation of the streets in this neighbourhood being admirably adapted for the purpose of the mutineers.

As the little group of rebels and their prisoners turned the corner of a street quite close to the walls, the Kabul Gate itself appeared in sight, a short distance farther ahead, shrouded in smoke and flame, but still standing, with the cannon—the fatal cannon—drawn up, six abreast, about a couple of hundred feet behind the gate, their grim muzzles slightly converging, and aimed so as to sweep the entire width of the road directly the structure itself should be destroyed and the British should dash forward to the storm.

Between the guns and the gate the houses bordering the street were already filled with sepoy sharpshooters, some posted at the doors and windows, some lying at full length on the flat roofs, their gun muzzles pointing downward, ready to open fire with devastating effect upon the foremost files of the British as they passed beneath. The ramparts themselves were crowded with men in red or grey tunics, all shouting their loudest, and apparently expending an enormous quantity of ammunition. The air fairly crackled with the sound of their volleys, even the broad daylight was illuminated by the continuous rifle flashes, and the atmosphere was so densely permeated with the fumes of gunpowder that breathing was not easy, even at a distance of a hundred yards from the gate.

Chaloner was gazing at the inner side of the massive gate as though he would compel his eyes to penetrate that mass of wood and iron, so that he might learn what success his countrymen were meeting with outside. Where, he wondered, was Nicholson, the indomitable leader of the assault? He would never allow the attack to fail; he might, at this very moment, be only a short hundred yards away, on the other side of the wall. Ah, if it were only possible to communicate with him, to let him know the desperate straits in which the men stood who had rendered it possible for him to deliver the present assault!

He was recalled to his present surroundings by Mehtab Singh's imperious voice ordering the sepoy guard to halt, and, glancing up, the lad saw that the place of execution had been reached at last.

There were the guns, their black muzzles grinning threateningly at the gate, the scarlet-coated, brown-faced sepoy artillerymen standing each at the breech of his weapon, a smoking linstock clutched in his right hand, while behind every gun was placed a brazier of glowing charcoal into which short iron rods had been thrust, so that the red-hot bars might be used to touch off the cannon should the linstocks smoulder out or be consumed before the proper time.

In the open doorway of one of the adjacent houses was stacked a pile of wide planks, about two inches thick, the purpose of which the two lads very easily guessed, seeing that several coils of thin but stout rope were also lying on the top of the planks.

The sepoy sharpshooters in the windows, observing three men, from their dark faces apparently soldiers of their own race, bound, and about to be lashed to the guns, shouted indignantly to Mehtab Singh to ask for what reason the men were to be punished. But when the sepoy general replied that two of them were *Farângis* disguised, that the other was a Sikh who had, as he called it, proved a traitor to the "Cause", and that the three of them were directly responsible for the attack then taking place on Delhi, they screamed and howled with rage, begged Mehtab Singh to hand them over to their own tender mercies, and even commenced firing at the prisoners themselves. Then the general, exerting his powerful voice to the utmost, informed them of the reason for which he had condemned the captives to die thus.

The men laughed and clapped their hands like children, crying that the *Farângis* would receive a pleasant welcome upon their entry into the city, and would know what it felt like to see their own flesh and blood blown to pieces.

"Tie a label to them, saying that they are *Farângis*," screamed one of the sepoys, "otherwise their friends may not recognize them!"

And, amid peals of raucous laughter, two of the grinning guard ran off to fetch the materials to carry out the suggestion.

"Cheerful set of jokers, aren't they?" observed Chaloner, watching the men who were bringing forward the necessary planks and ropes. "But perhaps, after all, it is not such a bad idea to label us. It will at least identify us, and show Nicholson that we died doing our duty; otherwise, as they say, it might perhaps be a difficult matter to recognize us—afterwards. They seem pretty certain in their own minds, by the way, that Delhi is going to fall, don't they?

"Well, here they come, old fellow," he went on, as the sepoys began to come up with their burdens; "we had better say goodbye now, I think. It will be our last chance. Poor old Shere Singh is still unconscious, I see, lucky man! It is to be hoped he will remain so, then he will never know what killed him. Goodbye, Fairbanks, old chap!" he concluded, touching his friend's bound hands with his own. "We have had good times together as well as bad, and we die in a good cause. If it should so happen, by any unheard-of chance, that you escape and I do not, let my people in England know, won't you? And, if the reverse should happen, I'll do the same by you. But I do not anticipate anything of the sort."

"Neither do I," agreed Fairbanks; "but of course, Peter, if it should so turn out, I shall most certainly do as you ask. Goodbye, old boy! our death will be a quick one, that's a consolation anyway. Why—good heavens, Peter!" he added suddenly; "it surely cannot be—and yet—— Look, man! who's that? Who's that fellow with his hands bound, who's being dragged along by that party of *sowârs* yonder?"

Chaloner wrenched himself from the clutches of the sepoys who had just seized him in order to secure him to a wooden plank preparatory to lashing him to the gun-muzzle, and gazed in the direction in which his friend was looking.

About a hundred yards distant was approaching a squad of mounted *sowârs*, their swords drawn, and in their midst walked a man, his wrists bound together and secured to one of the troopers' saddles with a short length of rope. That man's face was dark, like their own, like those of the men whose prisoner he was, but it did not look like a natural complexion, for it was strangely mottled, as though some of the pigment had worn off in places. He was wearing what looked like the very last remnants of a British infantry uniform, but it was so tattered it might have been almost anything.

It was the face, however, that puzzled Chaloner. He felt sure he had seen the man before, somewhere; but where——

"Hi! *Williamson, Williamson!*" he shouted, struggling in the arms of the exasperated sepoys, "how the dickens did you get here? We thought you were miles away."

The next instant he was hurled to the ground, and a couple of sepoys forced his back and shoulders against one of the planks in spite of his desperate resistance, binding him in position with a long piece of stout rope.

But although he could no longer see the English officer, he could hear his voice replying cheerfully: "Hallo! that's my friend Chaloner speaking, or I'm a Dutchman! And there's Fairbanks too. Where *is* Chaloner, anyhow? We are all in the same boat again, after all, it seems to me."

The irrepressible young man's voice acted like a tonic upon our two friends. That a man could be so cheerful in the face of death seemed almost uncanny, but its effect on Chaloner and Fairbanks was such as to make them feel that, after all, in spite of present circumstances, all hope was perhaps not yet dead.

As soon as Chaloner had been firmly secured to his plank, and was unable to move hand or foot, he was lifted into an upright position and the plank was tightly lashed to the gun muzzle with ropes. In this position, by turning his head, he was able to see that, meanwhile, Fairbanks had been treated in the same fashion, being bound to the cannon standing beside his own. Williamson, still wearing a cheerful smile at meeting his friends, was being tied to the weapon next in line, alongside Fairbanks, while Shere Singh, limp and senseless, was being fastened to a plank on the ground, preparatory to being secured to the fourth gun.

"It wouldn't sound kind," shouted Chaloner to Williamson, "to say that I'm glad to see you, considering the predicament we are all in, but you know what I mean. How does it come about that you are in this mess as well? We heard from Miss Graham that you had both been captured, but, as she didn't know where you were, we hoped that you had escaped again."

"Heard from Miss Graham?" echoed Williamson, his face brightening still more. "Is she yet alive then? Those scoundrels yonder told me she was dead!"

"She was alive six hours ago," answered Fairbanks; "but I am not at all sure whether she is fortunate or not. She is in the hands of that demon, Abûl Bûkr, the prince."

Williamson gritted his teeth and strained at his bonds until the veins on his forehead stood out like cords. Then, realizing the futility of struggling, he ceased his efforts, and presently regained his self-control.

"Poor girl! poor girl!" he muttered beneath his breath.

Then, aloud: "How did I get here, you ask? Well, it's a long yarn, but, briefly, it was like this. We got clear away, and were within sight of Agra when we were ambushed by a party of men of the Oudh Irregular Horse. Miss Graham was seized and placed in a palanquin, and that was the last I saw of her. I was bound hand and foot and brought here, then imprisoned in the fort. While there my jailers told me Miss Graham had died from poisoning in this very city, where it seems they brought her, too, unknown to me.

"One evening, by a stroke of luck, my jailer got drunk, and when he entered my cell I knocked him senseless, bagged his keys, put his cloak over my uniform, and slipped quietly out. I went straight to the Collector's house, hoping to find you there.

"Instead, I walked into the arms of a party of sepoys headed by Chunder Lâl and a man named Yusuf. At first they thought I was one of themselves, and I nearly scrambled out of that mess; but suddenly Chunder Lâl recollected that the face of the Mohammedan bridegroom, on the day of the feast of Hanumân, and mine were very similar. After that it was all up. I was collared, sent to another prison, and—here I am, butchered to make a beastly Sepoy holiday.

"But, buck up, you two, and look cheerful, or these fellows will think we're funking it."

Accordingly, Chaloner and Fairbanks "bucked up", and looked their tormentors in the face unflinchingly, in spite of the horrible jests and insults which they were compelled to endure.

What astonished them considerably was the fact that Mehtab Singh appeared to be waiting for something. He was pacing up and down in front of the guns impatiently, and constantly questioning the *havildar* in charge of the guard, the replies of the latter apparently not being satisfactory. Besides, a group of sepoys holding a plank and some ropes were standing beside the fifth gun, talking rapidly in low tones; and once or twice, during a lull in the tempest of fighting, Chaloner thought he caught the name of Chunder Lâl.

Then presently he heard a *sowâr* close beside him, who was leaning on the barrel of the gun, say to the sepoy artilleryman: "*Aur eck nai hai?* (Is there not another one?)" And he realized that evidently a fifth victim was expected to put in an appearance.

Could it be Chunder Lâl, he wondered, who had somehow fallen into disfavour? The men were undoubtedly speaking about him, and he told himself that he would die a great deal easier could he but be sure that the spy was to die as well, and so be prevented from sending any more good men to their death.

Meanwhile the uproar, the deafening rattle of musketry and the heavier booming of cannon, increased, if such a thing were possible, until one might have believed that the very gates of the Pit had been opened, or that the earth itself was being dissolved into its elements.

And still the Kabul Gate remained unstormed.

Then the doomed Englishmen heard a roar of execration from the sepoys around them, and, twisting their heads so as to look behind them, perceived the cause.

Half a dozen mutineers, their swords sloped over their

shoulders, were coming down the street at a quick step, leading, or rather dragging, another prisoner with them; and as Chaloner and Fairbanks recognized who the raving, protesting victim was, they were lost in amazement; for the man was none other than the mutineer officer and one-time friend of Mehtab Singh himself, Fuzl Aziz! And the man walking free beside the sepoys, the man with the smile of a demon distorting his cruel, cunning features, who was he?

The Englishmen looked closer, more fixedly, scarcely able to credit their senses, for the man with the triumphant, wicked smile was Chunder Lâl! Surely this was indeed a day of surprises, this last the biggest of all. Fuzl Aziz was the very last man they would have expected to see in a situation such as this. What on earth did it all mean?

The mutineers at once proceeded to lash Fuzl Aziz to the muzzle of the fifth gun, and, as they did so, Chunder Lâl, grinning like a ghoul and quite unable to remain still under his diabolical glee and excitement, was dancing about in front of his victim, heaping the vilest epithets upon the struggling man's head, and taking a spiteful pleasure in describing what he hoped would be Fuzl Aziz's sensations at the moment of death, as well as his sufferings in the Hindu hereafter. In fact, so utterly outrageous did he presently become, in the virulence of his hatred, that Mehtab Singh, who seemed to possess a few ideas of decency, seized the howling, capering creature by the shoulders, turned him round, and sent him spinning half a dozen yards away upon his face, with a single well-directed kick.

The spy picked himself up, and, with a vindictive glance at the sepoy general, hobbled up to the gun to which Chaloner was secured, and commenced talking in a low tone to the artilleryman in charge of it, who was evidently a close friend of Chunder Lâl's; and, by listening carefully, the Englishman was in a few minutes in possession of the facts of the case.

Some time previously, and shortly before the outbreak of the Mutiny, it appeared, Chunder Lâl's brother, a *saïs* (native groom) in the service of an English officer, had been selected as a messenger to carry round among the various British posts a secret proclamation calling on the native regiments to rise upon a certain date. This document in due course passed into Fuzl Aziz's hands for the purpose of being read by him to the men of his regiment; but, before he found an opportunity to do so, he became intoxicated, and either lost it or had it stolen. In order to keep himself out of trouble he swore that the *saïs* had never given him the paper, but had betrayed his countrymen by selling his information to the British, Fuzl Aziz being cunning enough to know that whoever had stolen or found the document would almost certainly try to sell it to the first officer he came across.

Fuzl Aziz's statement was believed, and the unfortunate *saïs* was seized and secretly put to death under circumstances of the utmost barbarity, as a warning to other "traitors". Before his death the unfortunate man contrived to inform Chunder Lâl of the true facts, and the latter then vowed to avenge his brother. He had therefore entered Fuzl Aziz's service as a spy, after the outbreak, and had gradually woven round him a net in the fashion that only a Hindu can. The crisis had occurred only a few hours before, while Fuzl Aziz was still unconscious from Chaloner's blow.

Chunder Lâl had accused the man of selling information to the British, and produced forged evidence to prove it.

That was sufficient; and now Fuzl Aziz stood, foaming at the mouth and exhausted by his struggles, lashed to the muzzle of a gun, the bitterest part of his punishment lying in his own knowledge that he was entirely innocent of the particular crime for which he had been condemned to suffer.

As the spy concluded his narrative in oily tones, Chaloner almost resolved to call up Mehtab Singh and tell what he had overheard. Then it occurred to him that a statement by an Englishman that Fuzl Aziz was not guilty would only serve to compromise the unhappy wretch more deeply, and he held his peace.

And now it really appeared as though the end was not to be long delayed. Rolling volleys of musketry, fired but a short distance outside the gate from the sound of them, announced the fact that, in spite of the desperate resistance being offered by the defenders, the British attacking-force was creeping up nearer and nearer to the fatal gate. The sepoys themselves had congregated for the most part on that portion of the ramparts adjoining the bastion, directing a galling fire upon every attempt to rush the drawbridge and reach the Kabul Gate itself. But the closeness with which the men were packed exposed them to considerable loss from the British rifles and field-pieces, and men were constantly being sent aloft to take the places of the shot-torn corpses which were continually being flung from the top of the wall by their living comrades, who found themselves becoming greatly hampered by the dead. The reserves of men drawn up behind the six sepoy guns for this very purpose were being constantly called upon, and their ranks were thinning fast; while, instead of being repulsed, the British were attacking more determinedly than ever, and Chaloner shuddered when he thought of the carnage that must be taking place among the troops.

He could hear the men cheering, however, and there seemed no despondent note, no diminution of confidence or determination, in those deep-throated savage shouts, the shouts of men who had heard of the Cawnpore massacre and meant whole-heartedly to avenge it. In addition to the ringing cheers he could also hear the heart-stirring skirl of the Highlanders' bagpipes, as the pipers played the regiments into battle, a sound which warmed the gallant Scotsmen's blood, and made them fight like furies. At times, too, could be heard the shrill war-chant of the Gurkha and Pathan levies—terrible fighters these—as they strove to outvie their white brothers in the energy of their attack.

And was not Nicholson himself at their head?

Oh! it was good; it was a fine thing to be a Briton, the lad told himself, his blood tingling with enthusiasm.

Tied to the muzzle of a gun, surrounded by a hundred thousand savage foes, staring death in the face, he could still be proud of his country; could still say that even his short life had not been lived in vain, since he had been privileged to fight in Britain's battles. Afraid to die? Rather was he proud to think that he would have the honour of being named among those who died on that splendid 14th of September which was to see the fall of the proudest city of India, the very stronghold of the mutineers' power.

Suddenly there arose from the ramparts a yell of concentrated terror, and Chaloner, glancing upward, saw that, while a number of the sepoys were redoubling their fire, directing it apparently at the drawbridge leading to the gate—or rather at the makeshift for one which the British themselves had placed in position with incredible loss of life—others of the men were scrambling down the narrow stairs leading from the ramparts, casting away their empty muskets as they ran, while some were even flinging themselves headlong from the walls upon heaps of dead below, in their anxiety to escape.

Escape what? wondered Chaloner.

Escape what? was Mehtab Singh's question also apparently.

With a word to the artillerymen standing behind each of the five guns, like animated bronze statues of Fate, the General, sword in hand, dashed up to the panic-stricken men who were streaming down the steps, showering imprecations on their heads for a crew of mutinous, cowardly dogs, trying to beat them back with the flat of his sabre—in one or two instances losing his temper and using the edge—and, between blows of his weapon, demanding to know, in the name of all the gods of Ind, what was the matter, what was the cause of the panic.

He might have saved himself the trouble.

The sepoys, utterly demoralized, would not stay to answer.

Avoiding the strokes of the flashing *tulwâr*, or turning it aside with their bare hands and arms, the men dodged out of the way of their infuriated officer, and, having reached the street, took to their heels and ran for their very lives, shouting in horrified tones something unintelligible to the bewildered sharpshooters posted at the windows of the houses, who in their turn exhibited signs of becoming panic-stricken.

Then, suddenly, the reason for their fright became apparent.

A second or two previously the silvery tones of a British bugle had rung out, high and shrill above the infernal din of battle, and, like magic, the crashing British volleys had died away, the cheering ceased, and even the skirling pipes ceased their clamour.

An instant later Chaloner, his eyes glued to the inner side of the Kabul Gate, wondering what was coming, was almost blinded by a white-hot flash of light which seemed to spring upward from the bottom of the gate in a funnel-shaped mass, like the first appalling outburst of a volcano.

The flash was followed immediately by the hideous roar of the accompanying explosion, which nearly shattered the ear-drums of the prisoners and their guards. The very earth appeared to rock, and the gust of wind caused by the explosion of over a quarter of a ton of gunpowder literally swept many of the sepoys off their feet, hurling them to the ground in all directions, while in the midst of the fire the massive gate heaved itself bodily upward in the middle, where the two wings joined, then flew into fragments, the pieces of wood, iron, and stone being whirled heavenward on the crest of the mushroom-shaped column of smoke which billowed up into the hot, shimmering air.

Not only inanimate objects were they which were hurled aloft in the cloud of smoke, but also hideous relics of what, a few seconds previously, had been warm, living flesh and blood, the mangled remains of those sepoys who had stayed by their posts on the wall, firing at the enemy until the last moment; and with them the shot-torn bodies of the gallant Britions who had fallen in the act of placing the fatal powder-bags against the gate.

CHAPTER XV

The Storming of Delhi

THEN ensued a brief period of utter silence, as though both the contending parties stood aghast at the fearful havoc caused by the explosion; and in that silence Chaloner and his friends distinctly heard the rattle and clash as the two shattered halves of the wrecked gate—a mere foot's width of splintered timber and iron—settled back on the torn and twisted hinges. Then through the gap left by the destruction of the gate could be distinctly seen the serried columns of the British storming-party, muskets levelled at the "charge", bayonets glittering in the sun, and colours flying; held like a hound in a leash, waiting for the word of command which should send them racing over the ground, across or through the dry ditch surrounding the walls, and in through the shattered gap to the storm of the city, to the vengeance for which they had all so long been impatiently waiting.

A moment afterward, while still gazing longingly at the liberty which was so near and yet so far, Chaloner heard the deep, whirring rush of air which told him that the upflung debris of the gate was now hurtling earthwards, and he instinctively shrank himself as close to the muzzle of the cannon as he could, expecting to have his brains dashed out by some falling mass of wood or iron.

One great piece, part of the huge cross-timber forming the sill of the gate, fell across the breech of the gun to which Williamson was lashed, dashing itselt into splinters and killing the artillerymen behind the piece, while the weapon itself was tilted skyward, the Englishman's body still suspended from the muzzle, and the priming was of course swept from the vent.

Another smaller fragment struck Mehtab Singh on the shoulder, breaking his arm and dashing him senseless to the ground just as he was rushing back from his futile effort to check the panic; while one of the great iron straps which had served to hold the timbers of the gate together plunged, end-on, down on the flat roof of one of the adjacent houses, penetrating the flimsy lath and plaster and killing five of the sepoy sharpshooters stationed at the upper window.

Other fragments fell among the crowd of fugitives, killing one or two; but, on the whole, very little damage was done by the falling debris, the British storming-party having been halted, by the bugle-note Chaloner had heard, just outside the danger zone. Most of the casualties had occurred among the men on the ramparts and among those who were firing through loopholes cut in the gate, and were due to the actual explosion itself.

Then, while the three Englishmen were still not quite certain whether they were dead or alive, the bugle shrilled out loudly once more, a high, triumphant note, and Chaloner saw the motionless red ranks quiver, like corn before the wind, while the forest of bayonets flashed back the burning sun-rays.

Another bugle-call, a quick arpeggio, sounded, and the straining ranks moved forward, as though every man were actuated by the same spring, and the bagpipes once more skirled out merrily, while this time they were joined by the massed bands of the British regiments, playing a little distance in the rear, near the Kishengarh Gardens.

It was a magnificent, soul-stirring sight to witness those bronzed, rugged men rushing grimly to the storm, every single soldier hard as nails, tough as whipcord from constant work in that hard country, every man's heart filled with the absolute certainty of conquest and the resolve amply to avenge the insults and atrocities that had been committed on their brothers and sisters by the swarthy demons in Delhi and elsewhere. On they came, their ranks firm and solid, absolutely unbroken by the fire that was still being poured into them, men leaping forward to take their comrades' places when they fell, without a second's hesitation. Nearer and nearer they swept, pressing unfalteringly after their officers, stern determination stamped on every bearded countenance, while the defending sepoys in the city felt their hearts turning to water as they watched that steady, indomitable advance, relentless as death itself.

Chaloner was aroused from his enraptured observation of the oncoming troops by hearing a sneaking, oily voice behind him suddenly remarking: "Say, brothers, have ye not forgotten these? Our general has fallen, but that is no reason why we should not carry out his orders. Surely ye do not intend to wait until the *Farângis* have entered the city, set these men free, and put you in their place? There is yet time to do what should be done. See ye to it!"

There was no mistaking the voice. It was that of Chunder Lâl. Chaloner, not having heard anything from him for some minutes, had been hoping that he was dead—killed by a piece of the falling debris; but, unhappily, he was still alive, and as vindictive as ever.

A hoarse growl arose from the artillerymen in response, and the captive Englishmen gazed at one another, said a mute farewell with their eyes, and braced themselves to meet their fate like men.

"*Dohai! dohai!* Justice! justice." yelled Chunder Lâl, wringing his hands in an ecstasy of rage and apprehension as he watched the rapid approach of the stormers. "As Buddha lives, let them not escape! Oh, hasten, hasten, or ye will be too late! May Kali, the mother of Slaughter, seize ye if ye fail to slay that dog of dogs, Fuzl Aziz. See, let me help ye," he fumed breathlessly, running to assist the artillerymen who were striving to depress the muzzle of the gun to which Williamson was bound, and which had been struck by the timber. "The elevating-screw has become bent," he howled, leaping up and down like a madman. "Run, run, ye sons of burnt fathers, and bring an iron bar. We will either straighten or break it. Hasten, or the infidels will be upon us."

"Another short respite," groaned Chaloner, as the gunners ran to do Chunder Lâl's bidding. "Would to heaven that they would be quick and get it over, for this strain is enough to make the stoutest nerves give way. But, by Jingo," he went on under his breath, "if they are not quick about it they *will* be too late after all! If those fellows yonder only knew the fix we're in, I believe they could save us even now."

"Those fellows", the charging storming-party, as it happened, did, at that very instant catch sight of the row of cannon pointing directly at the gate, with five men lashed to the muzzles, and they uttered a yell that might have been heard almost to the other side of Delhi. A tall, black-bearded officer, none other than Nicholson himself, also saw, and, waving his sword above his head, shouted to his men to follow.

They all responded nobly, straining every nerve to keep up with their gallant leader; but a few of the longer-limbed men began to draw away from the main body, and presently Chaloner fixed his eyes upon a compact little party of red-coats flying across the ground at racing speed in spite of their heavy kits and the intense heat.

Chunder Lâl and his men were evidently having more trouble than they had anticipated over the refractory gun, for the sepoy sharpshooters at the windows of the houses suddenly set up a howl that the *Farângis* were almost upon them; suggesting that they themselves should shoot down the helpless prisoners before their friends could rescue them.

The spy, in accents of the most piteous entreaty, begged them not to do so. His entire life would be spoiled, he declared, if he could not himself superintend their taking off—especially that of Fuzl Aziz. And as he spoke the refractory elevating-screw gave way with a little squeak of metal, and the ponderous barrel swung earthward once more, bringing Williamson down on to his feet again with a jar that seemed to shake every bone in his body.

"*Now!*" shrieked Chunder Lâl; "now we are ready. Get your linstocks, brothers, and do your duty. But, if ye have hearts in your bodies, start from this end. Slay Fuzl Aziz first, I beseech ye!"

The gunners, observing the rapidity with which the British were advancing, began to lose their nerve. They were anxious to slay the prisoners, but if they waited to do so the chances were that they would not get away with whole skins themselves. In fact, it would not be possible; and their lives were valuable to those men, for there were still cities in India where no pestilent British troops were, rich cities, well worth sacking, where each sepoy's loot might make him wealthy for life.

They hesitated a moment. Then they dropped their linstocks, turned, and fled, followed by the mocking laughter of the men in the houses, who had not so much to fear.

With a cry like that of a wounded animal Chunder Lâl hurled himself upon the nearest linstock, seized it, and found that it had become covered with sand and been extinguished.

Trembling with hate and anxiety, he turned to one of the charcoal braziers, wrenched out the rod which had been heating, and ran madly to Fuzl Aziz's gun.

The priming had been jarred off by the concussion of the explosion at the gate, but the vent was still filled with powder.

He rammed the red-hot rod down upon the tiny hole, and the Englishmen, who had been watching, turned their eyes away, shuddering.

There was a peculiar, flat, smacking detonation, and splinters of board, ragged ends of rope, with other fragments of a more ghastly nature, mingled with the grape- and chain-shot, went whizzing into the wreck of the right-hand gate-pillar, the barrel having become slightly deflected.

Chunder Lâl, laughing like a maniac, advanced to the next gun, the one to which Shere Singh was lashed, while the sepoys up above howled to him to hurry—the *Farângis* were almost on him!

"Somebody shoot that black hound," suddenly rang out the lion roar of General Nicholson, "or he'll finish those fellows off before we can reach 'em!"

A dozen muskets were raised to the hips of the charging men, eager fingers coiled round the triggers, and a ragged volley flashed from the musket muzzles, while the bullets whistled round both Shere Singh's and Chunder Lâl's heads.

But, alas! they did not find their proper billets. They struck down a couple of the fleeing artillerymen, but Chunder Lâl was not touched. He uttered a yell of defiance and leapt forward.

The next instant the fast-cooling iron bar was applied

to the vent of the fourth gun, the same dull report echoed on the hot morning air, and the Englishmen knew that the soul of their gallant comrade had passed to its own place.

Chaloner bowed his head and closed his eyes, for Williamson's gun came next in line, then Fairbanks's, then his own. The finger of death was upon them all, and the lad found his lips moving in a prayer that he thought he had forgotten years ago.

Then the sharpshooters, unable to control their impatience any longer, fearing greatly that Chunder Lâl would not be in time, commenced to fire on their own account—some at the troops, in order to check their advance, and some at the prisoners—and the bullets began to whistle round the ears of the three captives.

"Fire again!" shouted Nicholson, as the head of the advance-guard swept over the ruins of the Kabul Gate; and a second party of men, who had reserved their fire, obeyed the order.

Chunder Lâl, fumbling with the iron rod, received one of the balls in his shoulder and dropped the instrument with a horrid imprecation. He stooped hurriedly to pick it up, and, as he straightened himself again, a bullet, fired by his own friends, and intended for Williamson, pierced his brain, and the spy dropped dead across the trail of the gun-carriage, his blood pouring over the powder priming of the vent, which in another instant he would have touched off.

A rousing British cheer caused Chaloner to open his eyes just in time to see the Hindu in his brief death-struggle; and he himself gave vent to a hollow croak that he thought was a cheer.

Fairbanks and Williamson, who had been gazing at the advancing red-coats as though fascinated, heard the sound, glanced at Chaloner's joyous countenance, and then twisted their heads round to learn the cause.

They could not see Chunder Lâl's body, for at that moment a swarm of their own sun-tanned, red-coated countrymen surged in upon them, crashing volleys of musketry were fired at their very ears, and then they realized that several pairs of eager hands were engaged in casting loose the rope lashings that bound them to the guns.

Nicholson himself, leaning on his drawn sword, came up and put a few hasty questions to Chaloner; while the soldiers, reinforced now by the second half of the storming-party, which had by this time arrived on the scene, were keeping up a hot fire on the closely-packed houses bordering the street, with the object of silencing the galling attentions of the mutineer sharpshooters.

A few seconds later the three young men found themselves free once more, standing in the centre of a compact body of soldiers whose bodies on several occasions received the bullets that were meant for the recent prisoners.

They lost no time in rubbing their stiffened limbs and muscles in order to restore the circulation; and five minutes after their bonds had been cut they were feeling as ready as ever to pit themselves against the foe. They had a good many scores to wipe out, and they were eager to do it.

Chaloner could scarcely repress a shudder when he realized that, had Nicholson and his men arrived but one short minute later, his fate, with that of Fairbanks and Williamson, would have been sealed. They had all had a very, very narrow escape.

The fire from the houses, owing to the deadly accuracy of the British volleys, had now slackened considerably, and Nicholson at once told off a few files of men with fixed bayonets to go into the buildings and clear out into the street any of the sepoys who were still alive, for he was eager to advance into the city itself, and it would be dangerous to leave any armed sepoys in their rear, however small the number.

Consequently, about half a company of Fusiliers dashed at the houses, and in a few seconds the shrieks, cries, and prayers for mercy of the trapped mutineers could be heard, as the red-coats grimly carried out their task. But the sepoys might as well have asked mercy of the cobble-stones in the street, for all the quarter that was allowed them.

The stern, bearded men, wielding their rifles and bayonets so savagely, had all heard of Cawnpore, the Bibigarh and the Well, besides other nameless atrocities, too numerous to mention, committed by the friends or relatives of these very men; and it was hardly to be expected that Britons, many of whom had lost their own wives and children in that hideous massacre, would listen to appeals for mercy from men who had shown very plainly that they themselves did not know the meaning of the word.

Meanwhile, during the work of retribution, Nicholson had been examining the ground in front through his field-glasses, and had made up his mind—assisted by Chaloner's latest information—what was the best course to pursue. It was necessary, he decided, to sweep the enemy out of the narrow streets fringing the walls, and out of the houses bordering the streets, before it would be safe to advance much farther into that city of teeming thousands.

A second division of his troops had been told off to storm the Kashmir Gate, and make its way into that quarter of the city, subsequently joining up with the division under his own personal leadership, if possible, after which the combined force would find itself strong enough to penetrate anywhere, and the occupation of the whole of Delhi could be proceeded with,

By the time that the last of the sepoys had been

driven out of the houses and shot down, or hurled out of the windows and dashed to pieces on the stones below, the three lads, who had been searching industriously, had managed to secure a serviceable sword apiece, as well as a revolver each, which they had borrowed from such of the British officers as happened to possess a couple, and were ready to go forward with the main body of the attacking force.

Then the bugle pealed forth, the stragglers, who were disposing of the last few mutineers, appeared from doorways and round corners at a run; the men formed up in column of fours, a spray of skirmishers was thrown forward a little, and at a word of command from Nicholson the column started forward, the General himself well in advance, waving the men on—not that they needed encouragement—while our three friends, eager as schoolboys, marched alongside the leading company-officers, the enthusiastic Tommies behind cracking good-humoured jokes anent the black faces of some Englishmen, and the piebald complexion of others.

Then suddenly, as the head of the column turned a corner, the whole of the cross-street appeared to burst out into flame, and a perfect hurricane of bullets ploughed into and through the British ranks, while a chorus of fiendish yells and cries of triumph told only too well of the trap into which the troops had fallen. The skirmishers, who had been allowed to enter the street unmolested, so as not to alarm the main body, were slaughtered to a man, and unmistakable signs of panic began to make their appearance among the soldiers. The blow was a crushing one, and had of course been utterly unexpected.

Nicholson saw the danger and grappled with it on the instant, like the born leader of men that he was.

"Men! men!" he shouted; "what are you about? Steady in the ranks, there; steady, I say! Are you going to quail before a little bit of punishment like this? I know my men better than that, surely. Come along, boys. Follow me! Are you going to let me carry those houses and turn those fellows out with my own hands?"

The answer was a deep, thunderous roar of: "We'll follow you anywhere, sir!" and the troops, already ashamed of their momentary weakness, surged forward, a living wave, in the wake of their brave leader; while the sepoys in ambush, hearing the deadly menace of that shout, began to wish they had not triumphed quite so soon.

A good many of them also wished that the houses possessed more and larger backdoors.

Away went Nicholson, his men close on his heels. But Chaloner, Fairbanks, and Williamson were a little closer still, inasmuch as that they charged beside him.

The British rifles now began to speak again, and the cruelly galling fire from the windows slackened; but, alas! there was something about to happen that made even the capture of Delhi seem too dear at the price.

One of the sepoys, a man named Kâleh Khan, had noted by Nicholson's dress that he was an officer of high rank, and had determined to endeavour to check the British advance by slaying their leader, in the hope that the men, seeing their officer fall, would become demoralized, and would retreat, after the fashion of his own countrymen upon similar occasions.

The fellow therefore loaded his musket with a heavy charge of powder, ramming two balls down on the top of it. Then, at the moment when Nicholson turned to cheer his men on, Kâleh Khan took a long, careful sight, pulled the trigger, and the heavy double charge struck "The Lion of The Punjab" full in the back.

Nicholson remained upright for a few seconds; then, as the Fusiliers swept up round him, his knees gave way, and he fell—or rather collapsed—into the arms of

Chaloner and Fairbanks, who had turned, upon hearing the shot strike and the General's involuntary cry of agony.

"Good heavens, sir!" gasped Chaloner; "are you badly hurt?"

Nicholson did not reply, but, raising himself slightly in the two lads' arms, he shouted: "Never mind me, men; do not stay on my account. Push forward," he went on, to his officers, "push forward, gentlemen. Remember that you have to clear this street. Don't let those rascals stop you. For Britain's sake, go on!"

So powerful and free from any trace of pain was his voice that his officers believed he could not be very seriously wounded, and, calling the men together, they dashed ahead to the storm, crying: "See that you pay the Pandies in full for your General's wound!"

They passed on, leaving Nicholson lying on the bare stones, his shoulders still supported by the arms of Chaloner and Fairbanks.

In a voice dry and harsh with anguish the wounded general asked for water; and Chaloner, who had no canteen, hastily procured one, taking it from the body of a slain British soldier.

Then, while Fairbanks strove to revive the swooning sufferer, Chaloner raced back along the street to where he had seen an overturned *dhooli* lying by the wayside; having found which, he dragged it, as well as he could, to where Nicholson was lying. When, handling him as gently as they could, the two friends placed the wounded man in the vehicle, and, drawing it to the roadside, out of the way, prepared at his own request to leave him. Before they went, however, Nicholson called to Chaloner and said:

"Mr. Chaloner, when the fight is over, find Colonel Chamberlain and say I sent you. He has something for you, the receipt of which will give you pleasure, I hope. And now, please leave me. I shall be quite safe here, and you can do nothing for me, while there is plenty of work still to be done yonder."

The General spoke with obvious effort, and he had no sooner finished than he swooned, so Chaloner lowered the curtain softly, to exclude the sun, and the two lads turned sorrowfully away.

They pressed forward along the lane, being eager to overtake the troops and secure their own share of the fighting, the sounds accompanying which could very plainly be heard a little distance farther on, apparently just round the next bend in the street. They were also anxious to rejoin Williamson, who, seeing that Chaloner and Fairbanks were staying behind with the wounded General, had pressed forward with the men, adding his own shouts of encouragement to those of the other officers, and acting in every respect as though he were one of the Fusiliers' subalterns himself.

The houses between which the friends were then passing, and which, a quarter of an hour previously, had been filled with *bhang*-maddened sepoys, thirsting for *Farângi* blood, had been thoroughly cleared; first by means of deadly, smashing volleys fired from the street, then by means of the even more deadly bayonet, wielded by the Fusiliers inside the buildings themselves.

Meanwhile the turmoil of strife had been growing louder and ever louder, and as the lads darted round the bend in the street they were just in time to hear the crash of three volleys fired one after the other, followed by a thunderous British "Hurrah!" and to see the mass of red- and grey-clad mutineers—who had left the houses in order better to dispute the passage of the streets—break, turn tail, and run for their lives, hotly pursued by the Fusiliers, who then proceeded to ply their bayonets with vengeful effect.

Panic began to seize the sepoys, and presently all

idea of resistance vanished. They threw away their muskets, even tore off their bayonet scabbards, and flung away their shakos in order to disencumber themselves of everything which might hinder them in their flight. They had put up a most stubborn resistance thus far, but human endurance has its limit, and the sepoys reached the limit of theirs long before the sterner, stronger races of the North.

Out of breath though the lads were, they managed to put on a little extra pace, and in less than a minute found themselves alongside Williamson once more, and took up their part in the game with great relish.

"How goes it with the General?" enquired one of the Fusiliers' officers, while binding up a long, ragged cut across the back of his hand and wrist. "Hope it is nothing serious?"

"I very greatly fear it is, though," replied Chaloner gravely, as he parried a vicious thrust and then cut his man down. "The General will never fight another battle; his wound is a mortal one."

The officer's jolly, red face went white, then flushed purple. Suddenly, leaping upon a pile of corpses and holding his dripping sword aloft, he shouted, in a voice that made itself heard high above the din: "Men, General Nicholson is dead—or dying! The bullet we saw strike him has killed him. Now go on and exact full payment for his life!"

For a brief second there ensued an awful pause, while men glanced, horrified, into their comrades' eyes. Then the Fusiliers gave utterance to a dreadful sound—like that of wild beasts scenting their prey—causing Chaloner's blood to run cold, and he shivered in spite of the terrific heat of the morning.

The news was shouted across to the Kashmir men, who at that moment came up, and the struggle was resumed in a fashion that even now sometimes causes

Chaloner to leap trembling from his bed of dreams, after the lapse of so many years.

The details of that fight in the streets of Delhi beggar description—indeed, are not fit to be described; and all that can be set down in print is the bare statement that, when all was over, not a single sepoy remained alive. There were not even any wounded Pandies, they were all dead. The first instalment of Britain's righteous vengeance had been taken.

After all was over, and the exhausted men were leaning on their rifles, or cleansing their ensanguined bayonets and swords, Chaloner went over to a tall, clean-shaven officer in staff uniform, whom he guessed could be none other than Colonel Neville Chamberlain.

"Are you Colonel Chamberlain, sir?" he asked.

The tall man looked keenly at him for a moment, evidently marvelling at the brown face under the cavalry turban, for besides Chaloner's own and Fairbanks's, and Williamson's piebald complexion, there were no brown-skinned men living in that particular neighbourhood. Indeed, all three of the youngsters had had many narrow escapes of being killed in mistake by their own countrymen.

"Yes, I am, young man," was the slow response. "What do you want? You are an Englishman, surely, are you not?"

"My name is Chaloner, sir," replied the lad, "and I was bidden by General Nicholson to ask you for a packet as soon as you had time to attend to me."

"Oh! So you're Chaloner, eh?" said Chamberlain, smiling, as he screwed a single eyeglass into his left eye. Then, holding out his hand: "I'm very glad to meet you again, young man. I saw you once, you recollect, in General Nicholson's tent; but I couldn't quite place you just now. Yes, I have a packet for you. Here it is. You had better open it and see what's inside."

Chaloner did so.

As his eyes took in the import of the document they grew wider and wider open, his jaw dropped, and he stood there the picture of surprise and astonishment.

"Bad news?" asked Chamberlain, with a twinkle in his eye.

"Anything but that," was Chaloner's reply. "It seems too good to be true; that's all. General Nicholson has promoted me to be captain, has given me command of the squadron of Multâni Horse that he himself had raised, and has given my friend Fairbanks a commission in the same corps as lieutenant. Even poor old Shere Singh is remembered; but, unhappily, he has not lived to receive his reward. Excuse me, sir; I really must go and tell Fairbanks the news."

And away the lad dashed to gladden his chum's heart with the tidings, for he knew that only circumstances had prevented Fairbanks from obtaining the desire of his heart—a place in the army—and that he had been obliged to become a telegraph clerk greatly against his will.

The news was just as enthusiastically received in this quarter, and Chamberlain, watching through his eye-glass, smiled, well pleased.

"They'll do well and go far, those youngsters," he said to himself. "They have youth, energy, enthusiasm, and health. What more could any man want? They are lucky young dogs."

That same evening Chaloner paraded his squadron, and, through an interpreter, read his commission, which was to be gazetted as soon as possible. The men cheered him to the echo, for his services and his gallantry had been more widely known than he had any idea of.

Then he dismissed the men and strolled over, under the splendid tropic moonlight, to have a chat with Williamson.

That worthy youth was not in his tent, and Chaloner was just on the point of going back to his own quarters when the missing man dashed up on a horse which he had ridden nearly to death; for, ere he could dismount, the animal collapsed, and Williamson was pitched on his head, right at Chaloner's feet.

"Hallo, hallo, hallo! what's the meaning of this?" demanded the newly made captain.

There was no reply. Williamson had been stunned by the fall.

CHAPTER XVI

Retribution!

WHAT the matter was could not be learned until about an hour after daybreak, when Williamson suddenly recovered his senses. He sat up on the *charpoy* upon which he had been laid, and passed his hand before his eyes.

"What's happened? What am I doing here?" he asked in a dazed fashion.

Chaloner told him.

Then the light of recollection sprang to his eyes and he leaped to his feet.

"Oh, heavens above!" he groaned, staggering blindly forward into Chaloner's arms. "What have I done? Say, Chaloner," he continued hoarsely, "how long have I been lying, a useless, senseless log, on that *charpoy*? Answer me! Quick!"

"Why," replied Chaloner, mystified, as he pushed Williamson gently back on to the camp-bed, "you have been unconscious for about—let me see—about eight hours. What's the trouble, eh?"

"Trouble! *trouble!*—Listen, Chaloner," he urged breathlessly. "We have all been criminally forgetful. Yesterday, when we were all tied to the guns, you told me that Miss Graham was in the hands of Abûl Bûkr. We could do nothing to help at that time, and afterwards we were all so selfishly thinking of ourselves only, occupied with the one idea of sating our own vengeance on the sepoys, that we forgot—may heaven forgive us! —the desperate straits in which that poor girl might be placed during all that time.

"Directly I remembered, I borrowed a horse and rode at full speed to Abûl Bûkr's palace, trusting to luck not to be killed on the way. I entered the place only to find it deserted, except for one or two half-crazy servants. But at the muzzle of my revolver they told me what I wanted to know.

"Abûl Bûkr had left directly he learned that both the storming-parties had been successful, taking with him all his treasure and a white woman prisoner.

"A strong guard had gone with him as escort, so I dared not pursue alone, and I was coming here for help when—well, you know what happened. And now that—that—demon has had ten or more hours' start, we do not know which way he went, and that unhappy girl will probably never be seen again. Chaloner, try to think of some way of saving her, for I cannot. My brain seems to be benumbed; it refuses to act."

"All right!" said Chaloner soothingly. "Don't give way, old chap. We'll get her back safe and sound somehow, I vow. Just let me think a moment; I'll soon find a way out of the difficulty."

Presently he said: "Look here, Williamson, Abûl Bûkr and his precious escort can't have gone far, seeing that he was taking all his treasure, and, more likely than not, a quantity of his household goods. I know these Hindus; they always travel slowly, and I'll bet he isn't far off even now. Come on; we'll ascertain which way he's gone, and I'll call out my squadron and go in pursuit."

And he literally dragged Williamson from the tent.

"Your squadron?" gasped the latter in surprise. "What do you mean? Have you——?"

"Here, don't waste breath asking questions," retorted

the captain of Multânis, "but come along. It's all right, I promise you."

A few moments later the bugle rang out in the Multânis' cantonments. "Boot and saddle" was the order. Williamson was provided with a fresh horse, and they were ready to be off.

As they clattered away, swords and bridle-bits clinking merrily, a horseman cantered up, clad in the uniform of one of the newly formed Irregular Cavalry regiments.

"Captain Chaloner?" he enquired courteously, saluting.

"The same, sir," replied the lad, returning the salute.

"I'm Major Hodson, of Hodson's Horse," explained the officer. "I've just heard that you're out after Abûl Bûkr and some lady whom the scoundrel has kidnapped. Is that correct?"

"Quite correct," was the reply.

"Then I beg that you will allow me to accompany you," said the Major. "I've just spoken with a native runner, who reports having passed Abûl Bûkr's company going south—near Humayun's Tomb. It is important that we capture the man, very important indeed, and I was going to take my own squadron. But, hearing that you and your men are on the same errand, I thought I'd save my fellows. They had a hard day yesterday, and I shall save time this way."

"Certainly, sir," said Chaloner heartily. "Near Humayun's Tomb, you say? All right, we have them then. They cannot get away. Squadron—trot!" he shouted, and off they went in a cloud of dust.

A couple of hours later Hodson, peering under the sharp of his hand, cried out: "There they are—not two miles away. See that dust, with the glint of steel showing in its midst? Those are they. We'll soon have that lady of yours safely back again, Lieutenant Williamson."

Williamson, his head bandaged, his face white with pain and anxiety, tried to smile, but the attempt was a failure, and they rode forward in silence.

Presently the cloud of dust in front resolved itself, not only into an armed escort of mutineer cavalry, but also into a vast crowd of Abûl Bûkr's servants, friends, relatives, and, in fact, his whole household as well. There must have been well over a thousand of them altogether, while Chaloner's force only numbered a bare hundred.

"Never mind," remarked that youth, "the more the merrier. We'll show 'em who's who. Come along, you Multâni lads, *gallop!*" he shouted.

At the sound of the pursuing hoof-beats, the officer of the mutineer lancers wheeled in his saddle—*and saw.*

The heavy wagons comprising the convoy rumbled forward more quickly as the drivers mercilessly lashed the tired bullocks, the huge crowd tried to get out of the way by edging in to the sides of the road, and Abûl Bûkr's guard, after a hurried examination of the Multânis, decided that they would prefer, in spite of their superior numbers, not to fight the lean, lathy northern men on the big horses.

Consequently, the guard kept their sabres in their scabbards, and the lance-butts were not moved from their slings. The horsemen simply sat still on their animals, glowering hatred at the men whom they would have liked to attack but dared not; and as the Multânis swept up at a gallop, they opened out sullenly and let the loyal horsemen through.

"Leave Abûl Bûkr to me, Captain Chaloner, please," said Major Hodson, "as well as his brother, Mirza Sultamet and the old king's nephew, Mirza Mogul, if, as I strongly suspect, they are here as well. I have strict orders to—er—to attend to these three men myself. You don't mind, I hope, do you? Meantime you can hunt up Miss Graham and see whether she is all right. Mind you let me know if there is anything in the least wrong," he shouted, as Chaloner started to ride off with the fuming Williamson and a score of troopers, leaving his chum behind to look after the rest, and to hold himself at Hodson's convenience.

"Best thing to do," observed Chaloner, forcing his horse through the scowling throng, who were muttering imprecations and handling their knives impatiently, "is to start right where we are now and search every *bylie*, *gharri*, and *dhooli* we come across. We shall be sure to find her that way. You, Gunga Das," he went on, turning to his Multâni *havildar*, "and your men keep a good look-out that none of these people attempt to drive off any wagon or carry off any palanquin. And do not allow any man to move from here until either Major Hodson Sahib or I give him permission.

"Now, Williamson," he said, turning to the lieutenant, "let us examine this *bylie* first, and search thoroughly; then go on to the next, until we find her."

Keeping a wary eye on the natives, Chaloner and Williamson went from cart to cart, raising the sun-hoods and looking inside; and it was the lieutenant who found her at last, bound hand and foot and gagged, in a palanquin to which his attention had been drawn, just in time, by observing a quartette of bearers trying to sneak away with it.

He shouted the news to Chaloner, who at once joined him, and when the girl was released they found to their great joy that, thanks to Their Highnesses having been pretty fully occupied in looking after their own affairs, and also to the more or less prompt pursuit, Miss Graham had suffered nothing worse than the indignity of bonds, a very thorough scare, and a little rough handling.

Her joy and thankfulness for her release and rescue were extreme, but it occurred to Chaloner that she seemed to be rather more grateful to Lieutenant Williamson, and also more pleased to see him, than she was to himself or any of the others.

He smiled and, requesting her to seat herself in the palanquin again, ordered the frightened bearers to take up their burden once more and carry it back to the spot where he had left Hodson and the rest of his Multânis.

As the little knot of whites made their way back, Chaloner suddenly heard a tremendous uproar proceeding from the spot occupied by Hodson; and, hurrying up, he found that, the Major having arrested the three princes, and having placed them in a *bylie* for transport back to Delhi, the guard, smarting under the indignity, had at last taken their courage in both hands and begun to attack the Multânis with the object of trying to effect a rescue. The rabble had also joined in, and were now trying to pull the troopers from their saddles in order to tear them to pieces by sheer preponderance of numbers.

Chaloner and his detachment arrived as a very welcome reinforcement, and soon there was quite a savage little combat taking place there on the Agra road.

Miss Graham's palanquin was taken out of the press and set down by the side of the road, Williamson and four troopers undertaking to guard it with their lives.

After a sharp ten minutes, however, the prince's guard drew off sullenly, and all might have been well but for the rabble.

Numbers lent them courage, and the fight ebbed and flowed round the *bylie* in which the imprisoned princes were lying. In fact, before long it became apparent that unless strong measures were adopted, and that right quickly, the little British force might find itself in considerable danger, for men were falling fast, the mob was becoming bolder, and the mutineer cavalry were showing signs of attacking afresh.

C 745

"IT WAS THE LIEUTENANT WHO FOUND HER AT LAST"

Then Hodson, as was his custom, cut the Gordian knot.

He has since been blamed for what he did; but those who went into the matter thoroughly at the time, and on the spot, acquitted him of all blame. Moreover, they added that, in their opinion, he dared not have acted otherwise than as he did.

Seizing his revolver, and standing to his full height in his stirrups, he shouted, in Ûrdu: "You see these men, your princes, lying in the *bylie* here? Take warning, then, and hear my words. If ye do not disperse and go your way, and that immediately—if another hand is lifted to attack me or these men—then will I slay these three, Abûl Bûkr, Mirza Mogul, and Mirza Sultamet, with my own hand, before your eyes. Choose then, ye people, which ye will do. The lives of your princes are in my hand, and, as I live, they shall die if you disobey my bidding. I have spoken!"

A low, threatening roar, the most terrifying sound on earth, the murmur of an angry mob, arose from the close-packed ranks, and matters began to look very black. Still, even then, things might have been well, might not have come to a crisis, but for one man.

He was a *fakir*, a fanatic, and, half mad with hate and rage, he shrieked: "Cowards that ye are, ye men of Delhi! Are ye not a thousand to a hundred? And yet ye fear them, yet ye will let them steal your king's children! Shame on ye, shame on ye, if ye do this thing! Rise against them, ye *kala sûr log*, ye *bhangi-log*; rise and slay them!" And the old man fell down foaming, in a fit.

But his words had produced their effect, and in an instant his hearers were at the loyal troops like wolves at a deer's throat.

Hodson saw that the time to act had arrived, and he acted.

Raising his revolver, unheeding the cries of rage, horror, and amazement that were hurled at him, the Major pressed the trigger with his finger, and Abûl Bûkr, the man who had rejoiced to see British women "dragged through the streets of Delhi", leaped convulsively to his feet, in spite of his ankles being bound, and then fell, a corpse, over the low side of the *bylie* into the road. A second and a third shot rang out, and the other son and the nephew of the "Last of the Great Moguls" each gave a convulsive shudder, uttered a gasp of agony, and collapsed limply among the straw on the bottom of the cart, shot, with unerring aim, through the heart.

Chaloner, Fairbanks, and Williamson stood aghast at the suddenness, at the ruthlessness, of the tragedy that had just been enacted before their wondering eyes. That Major Hodson had been in earnest when he had threatened to shoot the princes none of the lads had believed for a moment; they had thought it nothing more serious than a last desperate piece of "bluff"; a gigantic "bluff", certainly, but one which they had never dreamed that the stern, merciless-eyed leader of irregular cavalry would dare to make good. Yet he had not hesitated an instant when he found that no credence had been given to his threat. He had shown the Hindus once again, in the plainest possible manner, that what a Briton says he means, what he promises to do he does; and the lesson learnt by them on that day of tragedies has never been forgotten, either by those who witnessed the act or by their descendants, to whom the story was, of course, passed on.

In the north-west of India mothers still subdue their children—and the subjugation is very thorough—with the threat that, unless they are good, the great "Nikal-seyn" will himself come and look into the matter of their conduct. The *ryots*, or peasants, still believe that o' nights they can hear the hoof-beats of his famous Arab charger among the hills, as its dreaded rider once more patrols the country he used to love so well. He comes, they say, to see for himself, as he was accustomed to do in life, with his own eyes, that his "people" are behaving themselves, and his coming, so they say, always foretells war along the Border.

So it is with the name of Hodson Sahib, although not to so great an extent. His share, too, of the reconquest of Hindustan will never be forgotten so long as men have tongues to tell the tale, have ears to listen to it.

For quite an appreciable length of time, after the firing of the fatal shots, silence as of the grave held those hundreds of men in its thrall, and in all that vast concourse not a sound was to be heard, no word was spoken, not a man moved. It was as though every human being there had been turned to stone by some Medusa's head. So still was everything that the usually barely audible sighing of the palm-leaves, as the soft wind blew through them, could be plainly heard, and even the sound of a bell tolling in far-away Delhi came down the breeze, softened by distance to a faint but perfectly clear tinkle.

Then a woman in the midst of the throng, overcome by the horror of the scene, gave vent to a high-pitched, hysterical laugh, and fell fainting to the ground.

The spell was broken. Men found that they had been, all unknowingly, holding their breath for the better part of a minute, and a great sigh fluttered through the assembly.

Hodson and the three friends, as well as the troopers, had been expecting to meet a savage rush of men, maddened by the insult offered to the royal house, and they were prepared for it. Every hand was glued to sword-hilt or revolver-butt with a grip of steel; but the expected attack was not delivered.

Whether it was that the mob was cowed by the execution, or whether the people had become at last overwhelmed with fear of these terrible men who stopped at nothing, and themselves knew not the meaning of the word "fear", it is impossible to say; but they just seemed to melt away gradually, every man moving off by himself, walking with eyes fixed on the ground, like a person in a trance, without breathing a single word to another. The mutineer cavalry, what was left of them, spurred their horses out of the press and galloped off southward, toward Agra, that being the last that the British heroes of Delhi ever saw of them. Abûl Bûkr's train, his relatives and dependents, started the wagon bullocks off again, and the long, slow procession resumed its way toward the south also, a request to be allowed to take with them the bodies of the slain princes having been sternly refused by the inflexible Hodson. He had a use for those corpses yet, he said grimly to Chaloner.

When the last laden wagon had proceeded on its way, then, and not till then, did Hodson turn to Chaloner and say: "Captain Chaloner, will you now please order your squadron to turn and escort that wagon yonder back to Delhi?"

A little later on, as they were returning to the city at a walk, he turned to the young man and added: "Chaloner, there will be no need for you or your two friends to be brought into this matter. What has been done back there, behind us, was done by my own hand, and I will include the matter in a report of my own. You may be sure of one thing, however, and that is, your reputation will not suffer in any way through this morning's work. Quite the reverse, in fact."

Chaloner saluted, and the rest of the journey was made in silence, except for the low murmuring of the Multânis as they discussed the death of the princes among themselves; and a lengthy—and subdued—conversation, apparently on some very important subject, which was being carried on between Miss Graham and Lieutenant Williamson, who, on foot and leading his horse by the bridle, was marching by the side of the lady's palanquin, the sun-curtain of which was now raised. Neither of them seemed to be in the least disturbed by the presence of the four scowling but now very subdued bearers. They also both looked very happy; and, happening to glance upward at the same moment, Chaloner and Fairbanks, meeting one another's eyes, lowered them again—and smiled.

There is now very little more to tell.

The squadron escorting the bodies of the princes got back to Delhi early in the afternoon, and Chaloner took his men into camp for the rest which they thoroughly deserved after their very strenuous morning's work.

Hodson reported to Colonel Chamberlain the action on the Agra road, who in turn reported it to Sir Archdale Wilson, who was now in charge of the operations, Hewlitt, the senile old creature to whom the loss of Delhi was due in the first instance, having been superseded, and also requested to remove himself to some sphere where it would not be necessary for his own subordinate officers to be obliged to threaten to shoot him in order to prevent him from playing the coward.

It is on record that this relic of a rotten system of promotion was very glad indeed of the privilege to depart, as lately his life had been anything but a happy one.

Wilson, the Commander-in-Chief, thoroughly approved of Hodson's action, it is satisfactory to relate; for it was not until some time had elapsed that the propriety of his behaviour on that occasion began to be questioned. And, even then, the only people who did so were the civilians, the arm-chair critics, who, of course, always know so much better than the men on the spot what should, or should not, have been done.

The occupation of Delhi, owing to the enormous population, and the guerrilla warfare that ensued, was not absolutely completed until seven days after the city had actually fallen.

It was entered on the 14th September, and on the morning of the 21st of that month the place was once again securely in British hands, the fact being announced by a grand salute of guns fired from the citadel.

Nicholson, "the heroic Nicholson", as all his brother officers were accustomed to call him, lived, contrary to every expectation, to see the fulfilment of the task he had sworn to complete, and on the evening of the 22nd seemed, if anything, a little stronger, so that men allowed themselves to hope that he might even yet survive.

But all their hopes and prayers were in vain. On the morning of the 23rd, nine days after he had received his wound, after more than a week of intense suffering uncomplainingly endured, he passed peacefully away amid the tears of the whole army. His work was over; but it had been a man's work, magnificently carried out, and his memory will live enshrined in the hearts of all true Britons as long as Britain herself endures.

He was only thirty-six when he died!

He left behind him a splendid example, and it is Britain's proudest boast that so many of her sons have followed, and are still following, in the footsteps of that great man, that "great and glorious soldier", as John Lawrence himself was wont to call him.

Chaloner and his Multâni Horse—Nicholson's own men that had been—were allowed to take a last look at their dead leader.

"Their honest praise," Colonel Chamberlain wrote

to his friend, Major Becher, in a letter, "could hardly find utterance for the tears they shed as they looked on their late master."

What better tribute to his life, what prouder epitaph, could any man have than that?

After the funeral, Chaloner and his men were detailed on a "roving commission", to scour the country, in order to rescue and help any fugitive Europeans who might be in need of assistance, of whom there were pitifully many; and his and Fairbanks's adventures during the twelve months or so upon which they were engaged in this work, doing magnificent service, may, at some future time, be set down, so that those who wish may read.

The storming of Delhi was the first real British success of the Mutiny, as it was also the greatest, for it broke the back of the rebellion and shattered at a blow the re-awakening Mogul power.

Then came Lucknow, its gallant defence and its still more gallant relief, and men said that this was the beginning of the end.

And so it proved to be, for it was the last great struggle between our soldiers and the mutineers.

True, a species of guerrilla warfare was continued until 1859, but this was only the last spark of a great revolt.

It is the custom to speak of the Great Mutiny as one of Britain's greatest trials; and so, in a sense, it was.

But that trial brought its own reward, and that reward is with us to-day, even as the concluding words of this unpretentious leaflet of British history are being penned. We have reaped it on the blood-stained fields of France and Belgium, where thousands of our gallant and devoted soldiers, emulating the magnificent example of Nicholson, Chamberlain, the Lawrences,

Hodson, Baird-Smith, Havelock, Campbell, Outram, and many another splendid man fought and died for Britain, in the hour of her bitterest and extremest need, in the same heroic spirit that animated the gallant souls who fought and died for her in those glorious, splendid, terrible days of the Great Indian Mutiny.